T0360455

Postcolonial Feminism in Management and Organization Studies

The term feminism is often treated as a stable and universalizing politics and practice. For postcolonial feminism, the issues of interest are not only social and cultural inequalities in terms of caste, class, color, ethnicity, gender, and religion, but also historical, political, and geographical inequalities in terms of "Third World," "Global South," and "remnants of the colonial past." Postcolonial feminism pays nuanced attention to historical diversity and local specificity of feminist issues. This book draws upon the work grounded specifically in the context of India, Pakistan, and Bangladesh to demonstrate the plurality of thinking.

In mainstream management and organization studies, context is often understood as a present, static field. This book discusses how context is an important consideration for any management and organization study and for feminist studies in management and organization studies. It informs the way we need to understand context not just as "present" but also as "past." Postcolonial feminism highlights the historical roots and past privileges of a context that often gets overlooked in management and organization studies where context is mostly understood in the present.

This book highlights the contributions of women writers, poets, and activists such as Christina Stringer, Elena Samonova, Gayatri Spivak, Mary Douglas, Naila Kabeer, and Uzma Falak to postcolonial feminism in management and organization studies. Each of these women has engaged with writing that has the potential to enrich and transform understanding of postcolonial feminism in management and organization studies, making this book a valuable resource for researchers, academics, and advanced students.

Vijayta Doshi is Associate Professor of Organizational Behavior and Human Resource Management at the Indian Institute of Management, Udaipur, India.

Routledge Focus on Women Writers in Management and Organization Studies
Series Note

Given that women and men have always engaged in and thought about organizing, why is it that core management texts are dominated by the writing of men? This series redresses the neglect of women in organization thought and practice and highlights their contributions. Through a selection of carefully curated short-form books, it covers major themes such as structure, rationality, managing, leading, culture, power, ethics, diversity and sustainability; and also attends to contemporary debates surrounding performativity, the body, emotion, materiality and postcoloniality. Individually, each book provides stand-alone coverage of a key sub-area within organization studies, with a contextual series introduction written by the editors. Collectively, the titles in the series give a global overview of how women have shaped organizational thought.

Routledge Focus on Women Writers in Management and Organization Studies will be relevant to students and researchers across business and management, organizational studies, critical management studies, gender studies and sociology.

Morality, Ethics and Responsibility in Organization and Management
Edited by Robert McMurray and Alison Pullen

Affect in Organization and Management
Edited by Carolyn Hunter and Nina Kivinen

Postcolonial Feminism in Management and Organization Studies
Critical Perspectives from India, Pakistan and Bangladesh
Edited by Vijayta Doshi

For more information about this series, please visit: www.routledge.com/ Routledge-Focus-on-Women-Writers-in-Organization-Studies/book-series/ RFWWOS

Postcolonial Feminism in Management and Organization Studies

Critical Perspectives from India, Pakistan, and Bangladesh

Edited by Vijayta Doshi

Routledge
Taylor & Francis Group

NEW YORK AND LONDON

First published 2023
by Routledge
605 Third Avenue, New York, NY 10158

and by Routledge
4 Park Square, Milton Park, Abingdon, Oxon, OX14 4RN

Routledge is an imprint of the Taylor & Francis Group, an informa business

Library of Congress Cataloging-in-Publication Data
Names: Doshi, Vijayta, editor.
Title: Postcolonial feminism in management and organization studies : critical perspectives from India, Pakistan and Bangladesh / edited by Vijayta Doshi.
Description: New York, NY : Routledge, 2023. | Includes bibliographical references and index.
Identifiers: LCCN 2022054611 | ISBN 9781032053691 (hardback) | ISBN 9781032053714 (paperback) | ISBN 9781003197270 (ebook)
Subjects: LCSH: Feminism—South Asia. | Postcolonialism—South Asia. | Organizational sociology.
Classification: LCC HQ1735.3 .P67 2923 | DDC 305.40954—dc23/eng/20221115
LC record available at https://lccn.loc.gov/2022054611

ISBN: 978-1-032-05369-1 (hbk)
ISBN: 978-1-032-05371-4 (pbk)
ISBN: 978-1-003-19727-0 (ebk)

DOI: 10.4324/9781003197270

Typeset in Times New Roman
by Apex CoVantage, LLC

To my beloved family for their immense support and sacrifices

&

To the Critical Management Studies (CMS) community for their tremendous support

Contents

List of Contributors   xi
Preface   xiii

1   **Introduction: Postcolonial Feminism in Management and Organization Studies: Critical Perspectives From India, Pakistan, and Bangladesh**   1
    VIJAYTA DOSHI

PART I
Feminist Resistance to Subalternity: Deconstructing "Development" and "Social Responsibility"   17

2   **Naila Kabeer: Deconstructing Empowerment of Poor Women Entrepreneurs in Postcolonial Bangladesh**   19
    AFREEN HUQ

3   **The Continued Silencing of Gayatri Spivak's Subaltern: A Critique of the Elite Nexus of NGOs, Academia, and Corporations**   36
    RASHEDUR CHOWDHURY AND FAROOQ AHMAD

PART II
Exposing Neocolonialism in the Post-colonies: An Urge for Ethics of Care   53

4   **Colonialism Otherwise: Reading Uzma Falak's Kashmir**   55
    AYESHA MASOOD AND SADHVI DAR

5   Modern Slavery in Contemporary India: Addressing
the Elephant in the Room – Contributions From
Stringer and Samonova   72
SWATI NAGAR

**PART III
Decolonizing Management Education and Praxis
Through Postcolonial Feminism**   89

6   The Epistemology of the Toilet: Doing Class Work
in Pakistan   91
GHAZAL MIR ZULFIQAR AND AJNESH PRASAD

7   Bringing Postcolonial Women Writers to Executive
Education: Case of Women Managers' Program
in India   106
NIMRUJI JAMMULAMADAKA AND PADMAVATI AKELLA

Index   122

Contributors

Farooq Ahmad (Ph.D., University of Southampton) is an independent researcher and a visiting fFellow at the University of Southampton. He has taught and undertaken research at several academic institutions, including Imperial College London and the University of Winchester. His research interests lie in institutional change, corruption, and professional identity.

Padmavati Akella is a freelance IT consultant and translator. She also shares a wide range of interests, including feminist and decolonial work.

Rashedur Chowdhury (Ph.D., University of Cambridge) is Professor of Business and Management at Essex Business School, University of Essex, and Batten Fellow at the Darden Business School, University of Virginia. His recent works focus on the Rana Plaza collapse and the Rohingya refugee crisis in Bangladesh.

Sadhvi Dar is Reader in Interdisciplinary Management and Organisation Studies at the School of Business and Management, Queen Mary University of London, UK. Her work contributes toward postcolonial and decolonial theory and activism in the field of business and management.

Vijayta Doshi is Associate Professor of Organizational Behavior and Human Resource Management at the Indian Institute of Management, Udaipur, India. She has published in reputed journals, including the *Asia Pacific Journal of Management, Gender, Work & Organization, Journal of Business Ethics, Journal of Business Research, Management Communication Quarterly*, and *Personnel Review*.

Afreen Huq is Associate Professor in the Entrepreneurship and Innovation program at the School of Management of RMIT University, Melbourne, Australia. Her work has been published in reputed journals, including *Journal of Small Business Management, International Migration,*

Women's Studies International Forum, Education + Training, and Higher Education Research and Development.

Nimruji Jammulamadaka is Professor in the Organization Behaviour area of the Indian Institute of Management Calcutta, India. She is the author of *Indian Business: Notions and Practices of Responsibility* (Routledge, 2017) and editor of *Governance, Resistance and the Post-colonial State: Management and State Building* (Routledge, 2017), *Workers and Margins: Understanding Erasures and Possibilities* (Palgrave, 2019), and *Managing the Post-colony: South Asia Focus* (Springer, 2022).

Ayesha Masood is Assistant Professor at Suleman Dawood School of Business at Lahore University of Management Sciences. She received a Ph.D. in anthropology from Arizona State University. She is interested in multiple aspects of citizen–state relationships and inequalities produced through policy design and implementation, especially administrative burden.

Swati Nagar is Senior Lecturer and Deputy Head of Department at the Department of International Business, Strategy & Entrepreneurship, Faculty of Business, Economics and Law, Auckland University of Technology (AUT), Auckland, New Zealand. Her current research interests include the Role of Gender in Modern Slavery, Migrant Worker Exploitation, and Challenges of Geographic Labour Mobility. She has published in several journals, including *AIB Insights, Palgrave*, and the *Journal of International Business Education.*

Ajnesh Prasad is Professor and holds the CRC in Critical Management Studies. His research interests focus broadly on gender and diversity issues in organization, interpretive methods, and social inequality. He has published some 50 journal articles in outlets such as *Academy of Management Learning and Education, Academy of Management Review, American Behavioral Scientist, Business and Society, Critical Perspectives on Accounting, Gender, Work and Organization, Human Relations, Marketing Theory, Organization, Organization Studies, Sex Roles, Sociological Forum, Studies in Higher Education,* and *Work, Employment and Society.* He is currently co-Editor-in-Chief of *Management Learning,* Associate Editor of *Gender, Work and Organization* and *Human Relations,* and Artefacts Reviews Editor of *Organization.*

Ghazal Mir Zulfiqar is Associate Professor in Public Policy at the Lahore University of Management Sciences, Pakistan. She is Associate Editor at *Gender, Work & Organization* and *Organization* and on the editorial board of *Human Relations.* She has published in the *Academy of Management Learning and Education, Human Relations, Journal of Business Ethics,* and others.

Preface

The book's genesis goes back to the *Gender, Work & Organization* 2018 conference held in Sydney, Australia. I was a conference participant and was fortunate to know of the exciting book series by Robert McMurray and Alison Pullen – "Women Writers in Management and Organization Studies." I was working on a project on postcolonial feminism during that time. I felt that the organization and management studies have a dearth of understanding of postcolonial feminism, especially from the context of a specific Global South – the siblings – India, Pakistan, and Bangladesh. With that proposal in my heart, I reached out to the series editors, who very generously became my mentors and guidelight. Without the encouragement and unwavering support of Robert and Alison and the persistence and openness of the excellent chapter contributors, this book would not have been possible. This book is a collective endeavor of ours. I am indebted to the Indian Institute of Management, Udaipur, and my research assistants for their tremendous support. The Routledge team has been very cooperative, patient, and helpful throughout the process. This book has survived COVID-19 (multiple waves). While it is a moment to celebrate, my heart goes out to the emotional turmoil and personal losses we may have faced along the way – my sincere and deep gratitude to everyone for keeping up with this project despite tough circumstances. Lastly, I am grateful to my beautiful family for their unconditional support.

~Peace, Love & Respect
Vijayta

1 Introduction

Postcolonial Feminism in Management and Organization Studies: Critical Perspectives From India, Pakistan, and Bangladesh

Vijayta Doshi

Postcolonial Feminism[1]

Postcolonial feminism is a way of knowing that brings together feminist (gender, class, color, race, and religion) and postcolonial (subalternity, "Third world woman/subject," "West and the Rest") concerns. Postcolonial feminism speaks from the spaces of those often positioned as marginalized "Others" and resists such domination through the inversion of the hierarchies of (neo/)colonialism and patriarchy (Gandhi, 1998). This is a project that critiques the domination of colonialism, neo-colonialism (imperialism[2] and capitalism), and patriarchy. Postcolonial feminism addresses the limitations of feminism without historical considerations *and* postcolonialism without gendered implications. Liddle and Joshi (1985) noted, "neither male domination nor imperialism alone accounts for women's subordination, but both act upon the gender division, and are linked in perpetuating women's oppression" (p. WS-72).

Postcolonial feminism is an attempt toward gendering colonialism and contextualizing and decolonizing feminism (Lewis & Mills, 2003). A postcolonial feminist approach is conscious of historical concerns and gendered and cultural processes, and structures. Within this intersectional synergistic relation emerges useful concepts such as "gendered subaltern" (Gandhi, 1998) and "postcolonial ethics of care" (Mooten, 2015) that expose and address power relations and allow nuanced and holistic analysis and understanding of past and present experiences. Postcolonial feminism attends to local feminist issues in postcolonial contexts, giving equal importance to the feminist phenomenon of interest as well as its colonial history and culture. Postcolonial feminist apparatuses enable creative and sensitive ways of doubling the force of dismantling oppressive historical and cultural structures.

DOI: 10.4324/9781003197270-1

Postcolonial feminism is a set of theoretical and political positions that employ feminist epistemologies sensitive to non-Western perspectives and contexts (Narayan, 2004). Postcolonial feminism has implications not only for ideation, conceptualization, and theorization of research but also for reflexively conducting fieldwork, for example, the positionality of a Western researcher in the field vis-à-vis the non-Western research participants (Özkazanç-Pan, 2012; Manning, 2021). Postcolonial feminist positions raise concerns over "for whom do 'we' produce knowledge?" and "what are the consequences of such claims of knowledge?" (Özkazanç-Pan, 2012, p. 582).

As Spivak argued, there is a need among the essentializing and universalizing Western feminist scholarship to "unlearn their privilege as their loss" (Harasym, 1990). According to Spivak, to unlearn one's privilege as one's loss means to trace how one's privilege (e.g., in terms of gender, Western identity, or ex-colonizer status) may prevent them from gaining certain types of situations and culture-specific knowledge (e.g., related to another gender, non-Western identity, or ex-colonized status). Several scholars, especially women writers, have contributed to the development of postcolonial feminist scholarship. It is important to read postcolonial feminism as wide-ranging approaches that cannot be narrowly defined, systematized, and of a unitarist theoretical nature.

In my own work on rural to urban migrant workers in frontline service work in India and women entrepreneurs in India (Doshi, 2020, 2022), I have been directly or indirectly influenced by the work of Chandra Talpade Mohanty (1988, 2003a, 2003b), Gayatri Chakravorty Spivak (1988, 1990); Min-ha (1989); Reina Lewis and Sara Mills (2003), and Uma Narayan (2004, 2019). In my own life, postcolonial feminism has come in many guises much before I knew such a term and phenomenon existed in the literature. I grew up in India. I was raised in Chandigarh, a vibrant city in the North, where people from many nearby states such as Haryana, Himachal Pradesh, and Panjab live. I was also exposed to cultural, religious, political, and language differences. While growing up in a middle-class family and attending middle-class schools, I witnessed demarcations between India and Pakistan (especially the Wagha border, cricket matches, and news on politics); women, men, and the third gender; rich, middle-class, and poor; and Indian- versus "non-Indian." During my doctorate and later at work, I got the opportunity to travel overseas for research conferences where I witnessed demarcations between India and "foreign countries"; brownness and whiteness; and developing and developed economies. Perhaps, this collection of experiences in the background illuminated some of my research projects and introduced me to the ideas of postcolonial feminism.

Here, I reflect on my identity and position as a postcolonial feminist researcher in the field of research and how it contributed to my relationship with research participants and the phenomena of interest. As a researcher, I have been interested in issues of gender, diversity, and inclusion for many years. Engaging reflexively during my fieldwork with the research participants, many of my research experiences spoke to me of the multiple identities of organizational employees. For example, one of my projects with rural to urban migrant frontline employees in shopping malls and the other one with women entrepreneurs, both in North-western regions of India, started as projects on gender. However, slowly, they have turned into projects on gender, class, modernization, and westernization in the postcolonial context of India amidst a globalized world (Doshi, 2020). I realized that feminism in the North Indian context, in which I have been researching, is unique from any other country because there is a history of the gendered and classed aspects of lived experiences of the people – a history that has had the masters/colonizers versus the servants/slaves/colonized. This relational superiority and inferiority have been passed on culturally and continue to exist within the organizations. The terms "modern" and "western" not only are status or locations but have a contextual genealogy of their own. The colonial power structures are not a thing of the past but rather resurface in the neo-colonial relations and are experienced by the employees in the organizations. The combined and enmeshed field research experiences garnered my interest in postcolonial feminism. Although the disciplines of anthropology, sociology, and women's studies have dealt with this idea for a long time, not enough has been researched in this area in the domain of management and organization studies (MOS), even though it is crucial.

Over time, as a management and organizational researcher, I have come to know that our so-called "corporate employees" may also be living with a postcolonial gendered/classed/racialized subjectivity. Likewise, the corporate cultures or contexts can also be illuminated and understood holistically through the postcolonial feminist approaches. Therefore, postcolonial feminism is as much an issue of management and organization studies as it is for any other discipline. Such an approach will only help the organizations embrace, understand, relate to, and support their "employees" and their "co-workers" in more meaningful, deeper, and holistic ways rather than dealing with a superficial transactional way between employer–employee or leader–team members.

Now, I reflect on my identity and position, not as a researcher but rather as an individual citizen of India. I often get asked by fellow Indians if I am Indian, given my different skin color and facial features. These experiences have continuously "Othered" me and rendered me colonized amidst the imperial "Indian looks" hegemony. In solidarity with other Indians of my native place and other "differently looking" Indians, I draw attention to the neo-colonial relations that the postcolonial neo-colonizers of the same nation have built for their fellow citizens. This phenomenon is different from the *Black Skin White Masks* (Fanon, 2008) experience, where the context was foreign (another country) to the author. In my case, the local becomes or acts foreign. Postcolonial feminism has the potential to sensitize us to the postcolonial neo-colonizing positions to evoke consciousness-raising and urge a sense of disengagement with the neo-colonial practices toward decolonization (Lugones, 2010). To this end, postcolonial feminism could be understood as resistance to local (as well as global) dominant forces. Thus, postcolonial feminism is a project not only to decolonize Western feminisms by bringing insights from postcolonial contexts but also to expose the colonial structures formed within the post-colonies.

The term "post" in "postcolonial" means the aftermath and not necessarily the end of fifteenth-century Western colonialism (Prasad, 2003). The term "postcolonial" used in this chapter suggests a way of thinking about colonialism and its consequences – it subsumes not only the past power relations between the literal ex-colonizing and ex-colonized nations but also its spill-over in the present neo-colonial forms of imperialism (such as capitalism) arising between the West and the Rest via cultural, economic, and political control (Banerjee & Linstead, 2004; Mohanty, 2003b; Prasad, 2003). Here, the colonial relations are not assumed to have vanished but rather are seen as imprinted in the history and culture of the colonized. Thus, I also use the term postcolonial to highlight the neo-colonial imperialist projects that arise and sustain themselves in new forms in the post-colonies. This book considers colonization as an event in history and relational power imbalances, some of which are persistent while others emerge and re-emerge in new forms. History and its current implications are important considerations here.

The term "feminism" in this book concerns social inequalities and marginality related to gender, class, caste, disability, race, religion, and sexualities. Significant concerns of feminism include solidarity, ethics of care, and collective resistance (Mohanty, 2003b). Cultural, political, and social relations are important considerations. Scholars have traced a convergent evolution of feminist and postcolonial theory wherein both deal with power relations arising from hierarchies at different levels – patriarchy and colonial authority. Despite mutual suspicion, possibilities of volatile partnership have been traced by postcolonial feminist researchers through the ideas of "third-world woman" (Spivak, 1988; Mohanty, 2003b), "special third-world women" (Min-ha, 1989), and "double colonization" (Gandhi, 1998). The inclusive vision of feminisms needs to be attentive to the postcolonial history and contexts and emerging neo-colonial structures. The inherent activist characteristics of feminisms also drive them toward decolonization.

Origin, Development, and Critique

The origin of postcolonial feminism can be dated to the foundational, influential work of Gayatri Spivak, especially her critical essay, "French Feminism in an International Frame" (Spivak, 1981). Spivak's concern was with the non-reflexive engagement of First-World feminist researchers[3] with the Third World women participants. She was critical and skeptical about the "colonist benevolence" of First-World feminist researchers in producing an essentializing and universalizing idea of Third World women as underprivileged, requiring rescue from their First-World sisters (Spivak, 1981). Spivak re-voiced her concern over the "re-presentation" ("speaking for") of an oppressed group in her essay "Can the Subaltern Speak"? (Spivak, 1988, p. 70). She used the term subaltern to refer to the oppressed and subordinated groups (in this case, the "Third World Women"). Spivak's dismay was the historically muted accounts of subaltern women. Simultaneously, Chandra Talpade Mohanty, in her essay "Under Western Eyes: Feminist scholarship and colonial discourses" (Mohanty, 1988), expressed her concern over the colonization of representation of third world femininities by the Western feminist writers and presenting a monolithic "third world woman." She urged for careful historically contextualized responses to complex realities.

Mohanty (1988) mentioned, "Sisterhood cannot be assumed on the basis of gender; it must be forged in concrete historical and political practice and analysis" (p. 68). Likewise, Trinh T. Minh-ha, in her book *Woman Native, Other* (Min-ha, 1989), reflects on the colonialist analytic category of "third-world women" and contends that third-world women have to articulate differences from the referent of Western feminism. Minh-ha, Mohanty, and Spivak express their concerns about the "double colonization" ("gendered subaltern" (Gandhi, 1998, p. 86)) of women under imperial conditions and misrepresentation of third-world femininities by the Western feminist writers and their disappointment over whether subalterns can speak for themselves. Minh-ha, Mohanty, and Spivak construct "western feminists-as-imperialist" in how a third-world woman is often spoken *about* rather than allowed to speak for herself (Gandhi, 1998). Later, Reina Lewis and Sara Mills (2003), in their book *Feminist Postcolonial Theory: A Reader* engaged extensively with the ideas of feminism and postcolonialism from multiple perspectives and different postcolonial contexts such as India and Algeria. Likewise, Narayan (2019) engaged in a postcolonial feminist critique of the contemporary Western feminist interventions into non-Western contexts, for example, the imperialistic nature of foreign-funded NGOs and their logic of "doing good" under moral and political obligation for non-Western subjects, often women. Overall, the ideas of postcolonial feminism have been to decolonize (western-centric/western-originated) feminism.

Postcolonial feminism has received its share of criticism. "Can only a black speak for black? Can only a postcolonial subcontinental feminist adequately speak for that culture?" (Suleri, 1992, p. 760). A vital consideration in the postcolonial feminist approach is the ethics of (re-)presentation (Spivak, 1988). The concern of seminal postcolonial feminist scholars such as Spivak and Mohanty was not so much about the authenticity or credibility of Western scholars researching and voicing for the non-Western women but rather the non-reflexive "re-presentation" of the stereotypic accounts of non-Western women even though out of concern and sympathy (Özkazanç-Pan, 2012). Postcolonial feminism is inclusive. For example, Manning (see Manning, 2021), an Irish women researcher, has lived in Guatemala and reflexively studied indigenous Maya women, thereby contributing significantly to the agenda of rethinking MOS as a Western-gendered system. Thus, critical ethical considerations in the postcolonial feminist approaches become not so much about who is researching but rather how (reflexively) one is researching: Whom are we researching? How are we presenting them? What implications does our research have on the present and future conditions of the participants and the phenomenon of interest?

Another critique of seminal postcolonial feminist work is: Is only the West hegemonic, or are there colonial power structures within the postcolonies too? Suleri (1992, p. 765) noted, "many Third World nationals bring the same kind of contempt and disrespect for blackness that is most frequently associated with white western imperialism." Lastly, postcolonial feminism has been critiqued for being divisive regarding feminism or postcolonialism. A similar argument can be made for any perspective that challenges the dominant rules of the game. For example, Bell et al. (2019) recently showed how feminist theory is seen as "dangerous knowledge" in MOS. Instead of perceiving postcolonial feminism as divisive, it can be understood as "dual forces" that advance feminism as well as postcolonialism, simultaneously.

Contrary to being divisive, postcolonial feminism is a call for pluriversality that encourages epistemic spaces and moves toward embracing different knowledges, ideas, and experiences from the Global South contexts and/or positionalities (Manning, 2021; Mohanty, 2003a). As Narayan (2004) writes, subaltern feminist epistemologies have an "epistemic advantage" or "double vision" from knowing the practices of both their contexts and those of their oppressors. Double vision, however, is not a celebration of exclusion nor a romanticizing of oppression (Narayan (2004); instead, it must be viewed as a means for decolonization. There are other forms of postcolonial feminist approaches from other parts of the Global South. For example, decolonial feminism in the context of Latin America (Lugones, 2010; Manning, 2021), or Africa (Nkomo, 2011) is equally important for the pluriversality of post-colonial feminist knowledge but is beyond the scope of the present book.

Advancing Postcolonial Feminism

Furthering postcolonial feminism, this book *first*, theoretically extends postcolonial feminism as not merely a critique of Western feminism but advances the knowledge of indigenous neo-colonial relations emergent within the post-colonies. Although postcolonial feminism originated as a critique of the global phenomenon of "the West and the Rest," the chapters in this book demonstrate how postcolonial feminism also deals with the local emergent power structures that shape and transform the post-colonies. It is a constructive advancement that captures the possibility of knowing different indigenous and local feminist issues in postcolonial contexts.

Second, this book advances postcolonial feminism by exposing neo-colonial relations in which, at times, the neo-colonizers are ex-colonizers; however, at other times, the neo-colonizers are ex-colonized themselves. Although this book shows both relational developments, it is the latter, neo-colonial structures emerging from within and between the post-colonies, which is novel, engaging, and insightful in this book for decolonization through postcolonial feminism. *Third*, the postcolonial feminist apparatuses of this book allow the consideration of issues beyond women *only* issues to include gender, class, caste, religion, sexualities, and other axes of differences. *Lastly*, this book provides a space for subalterns (the authors and the focal women writers) to speak, to be heard; and it demystifies them as subjects with their agency, voice, knowledge, and ways of working and organizing. The contributing authors for this book, irrespective of their current physical locations, are local or diasporic researchers with direct or ancestral links to India, Pakistan, or Bangladesh. Although some of the chapter authors may have been physically located in the West, as scholars, they could critique from within and write from their subaltern positionalities. They all are visible and ethnic minorities in their respective places of residence and/or work.

We may well ask: Why postcolonial feminism and not feminist postco-lonialism? Neither research nor researcher (choice) is value-free. I identify myself as a postcolonial feminist because the central research issues I have been interested in are around feminist issues of gender, class, and caste. However, I have faced a contextual handicap many times wherein postco-lonial contextualization provided me with a more nuanced, holistic, and local understanding of feminist phenomena of interest. Hence, the title post-colonial feminism. This book highlights that the postcolonial context and identity is a vital consideration for feminist studies in MOS; else, it remains an oversimplified or partial perspective.

Decolonizing Management and Organization Studies Through Postcolonial Feminism

There have been several studies on postcolonial theory and feminist theory separately in MOS (Banerjee & Linstead, 2004; Banerjee & Prasad, 2008; Bell et al., 2019; Calás & Smircich, 1996; Harding et al., 2012; Jack et al., 2011; Prasad, 2003). Although these are essential developments toward the decolonization of MOS, what has remained marginal and under-recognized is an integrated approach that allows simultaneous consideration of feminist and postcolonial issues in MOS. Postcolonial feminism is often mentioned in passing in both the postcolonial and feminist literature in MOS. By introducing postcolonial feminism in MOS, this book also suggests that some postcolonial feminist researchers are already at work within MOS "to dismantle/decolonize the philosophical tradition from inside rather than from the outside" (Spivak, 1988; Jones, 2005). Postcolonial feminism presented in this book considers the feminist issues beyond the debate of "third world women" and is also empathetic of the history and its implications in different postcolonial contexts. In doing so, it responds to the calls of some MOS scholars, such as Jones (2005) and Banu Özkazanç-Pan (2012), to advance the field of postcolonial feminism in MOS.

Marginalization of postcolonial feminism in MOS can be understood as "epistemic oppression," which perhaps arises from the "double threat" that postcolonial feminism presents to established ways of knowing in organization studies (Bell et al., 2019). Postcolonial feminism allows thinking from the perspective of "otherness." The mainstream literature in MOS is Western-centric in terms of theory and context and has thus colonized the field of management and organization studies. The mainstream MOS in the past have conveniently ignored the feminist issues in organizations and have presented organizational issues as ahistorical. This book offers MOS academia an opportunity for "unlearning of privilege" (Spivak, 1988) and rethinking "management and organization studies as a Western gendered system" (Manning, 2021). It directly addresses the geopolitics of (skewed/Western-centric) knowledge production in the MOS (Mignolo, 2011; Spivak, 1988) and allows knowing from the perspectives of gendered colonial differences. Further, it is not only the MOS scholarship but also the management and organizational education and praxis that is Western-centric and needs decolonizing. Speaking from the margins, in terms of both the theory (postcolonial feminism) and context (India, Pakistan, and Bangladesh), this book is itself an act of decolonizing MOS.

I consciously use the term decoloniz*ing* to emphasize that it is an ongoing process. Further, "de-colonizing" is more than anti-colonialism as it not only focuses on a critique of colonialism but also creates and shows alternate ways of knowing in post-colonies. Critical Management Studies (CMS) originated in the early 1990s created a space for postcolonial theory Many feminist, postcolonial, and postcolonial feminist researchers, work within the CMS community but not without its struggles. Postcolonial feminist research within the CMS has not grown at the same rate as postcolonial studies. This book shows students and scholars the potential of postcolonial feminism in MOS.

The analytical value of an integrated approach of postcolonial feminism in MOS is discussed through the works of Banu Özkazanç-Pan (2012) and Liddle and Joshi (1985). Özkazanç-Pan (2012) presented accounts of two Turkish women entrepreneurs and noted that a postcolonial feminist lens allowed an understanding of Turkish women entrepreneurs' "subaltern" positions in the global project of "high-technology entrepreneurship" and helped in challenging dominant US-based business discourses that impose the Western notion of self in "representing" Turkish subjects. In the absence of postcolonial feminist approaches, she found, the experiences of the Turkish women entrepreneurs would have been approached through either a "cultural comparison" approach or a (liberal) "feminist" approach. A cultural comparison approach to study high-technology women entrepreneurs cannot address global interconnections and dependencies [and historical relations], which produce inequality in the first place. A (liberal) feminist approach may call for action on behalf of women "over there" (i.e., Turkey) without considering women "over here" who are not in positions of power and privilege or the connections between "over there" and "over here" (Özkazanç-Pan, 2012, p. 580). Özkazanç-Pan's (2012) study critiques and advances postcolonial feminism to highlight neo-colonial/imperial discourses (West and the Rest) in entrepreneurship in the capitalistic context of the United States and Turkey despite the absence of a historical colonial relationship between the two. Postcolonial feminism can also be applied symbolically to imperial structures where the dominant/colonizer not necessarily took/takes territorial/physical control but economic, discursive, cultural, and political control over the subalterns. Thus, the postcolonial feminist lenses can also be used as analytical positions to unpack power dynamics.

An alternate way of applying a postcolonial feminist lens in MOS is to engage with the literal historical colonial relations to understand the roots of a phenomenon. For example, women's inequality and patriarchy in the context of India can be studied as a phenomenon with a colonial past. Liddle and Joshi (1985) tease out the link between gender and imperialism in

British India. They said, "The British used the particular form which gender divisions took in India as a vehicle for proving their liberality, as a demonstration of their superiority, and as a legitimation of their rule" (Liddle & Joshi, 1985, pp. WS–72). With the increase in participation of women in the workforce in India, women in organizations are being researched increasingly. Often, the starting point of studies is the gender inequality of women in India. However, unanswered questions remain: How did we arrive at the condition of inequality of women in the organizations in India? What affect did colonial history have on this phenomenon? Postcolonial feminist lenses will have a different starting point rooted in the colonial past to tease out a "contextual, local, and historical" understanding of a phenomenon. The various chapters in this book address and engage with either or both the postcolonial feminist approaches.

India, Pakistan, and Bangladesh: Collective Resistance

The focus on India, Pakistan, and Bangladesh in this book allows scholars and practitioners to organize collective resistance against common hegemonic structures. Postcolonial in this book means – Aftermaths of Western colonialism, more specifically, the British rule ending in India partitioning it into India, Pakistan, and Bangladesh. It was a critical phase not only because it marked the beginning of "post"-colonial phase but also because it had significant implications on the relationship between India, Pakistan, and Bangladesh – the three siblings who have experienced a patchy relationship ever since. The three countries had a shared history until British rule ended. Specific systems have persisted beyond the colonial control in the three countries. For example, the coloniality of the caste system cuts across the three nations even in today's times, and its spills over into organizations. Moreover, fault lines based on communal and religious identities within the three countries often cause unrest and disturbance in organizations. Further, the issue of a particular region of Kashmir remains a sensitive ongoing conflictual topic between India and Pakistan and has had human rights implications for civilians, especially women. These historical structures inform the postcolonial feminist lenses in the context of India, Pakistan, and Bangladesh toward coming together, respecting differences, to challenge the common hierarchies, social inequalities, marginality, and subalternity related to gender, class, ethnicity, race, and religion.

The focus on India, Pakistan, and Bangladesh teases out the heterogeneity in the "third world femininities" (Spivak, 1988; Mohanty, 2003a, 2003b) by privileging the subaltern femininities that are historically and culturally situated. Neither the "Third World" nor the "Global South" is treated as a monolithic category in this book. Based on local organizational issues in the postcolonial context of India, Pakistan, and Bangladesh, this book demonstrates how the local shapes particular knowledge structures and practices. The contents of this book, therefore, introduce to students and researchers the local postcolonial feminist issues in India, Pakistan, and Bangladesh. The collection has an underlying sisterhood intention of collectively improving the conditions of women and subalterns in organizations and society.

India, Pakistan, and Bangladesh are considered important "developing" economies in the world. Increasingly, more MOS research is being conducted in the context of India, Pakistan, and Bangladesh (Banerjee & Jackson, 2017; Crane et al., 2022; Munir et al., 2018). MOS increasingly recognizes these nations as "emerging markets" with a high potential for critical consumers, producers, importers, and exporters in the global economy. Not taking postcolonial feminist approaches ignores the history of a place, its gendered relations, and the contextual embeddedness (often reducing the contextual differences to "established" dimensions of culture (like Hofstede or GLOBE framework)). Whilst postcolonial feminist approaches can be used beyond these three countries, this book draws upon the academic work grounded in the context of India, Pakistan, and Bangladesh to demonstrate the plurality of postcolonial feminism.

Postcolonial Feminism and Women Writers in Management and Organization Studies

This book contributes to the book series: "Women Writers in Organization Studies" by highlighting the contribution of women writers and poets whose work has remained under-recognized and under-conceptualized in the postcolonial feminist literature in MOS. Even though postcolonial feminist literature readily acknowledges the work of seminal women writers such as Gayatri Spivak (1988), Chandra Talpade Mohanty (1988, 2003a, 2003b), Min-ha (1989); Reina Lewis and Sara Mills (2003); and Uma Narayan (2004, 2019), the work of women writers and women poets such as Naila Kabeer, Uzma Falak, Christina Stringer, Elena Samonova, and Mary Douglas has remained mainly ignored or under-theorized in the postcolonial feminist literature in MOS. Through the writings of a woman writer or poet, each chapter of this book illuminates a local issue and uses a postcolonial feminist approach to decolonizing MOS.

A Roadmap of This Book

This book has been organized around three themes, namely:

Part I: Feminist resistance to subalternity: Deconstructing "development" and "social responsibility"
Part II: Exposing neo-colonialism in the post-colonies: An urge for ethics of care
Part III: Decolonizing MOS education through postcolonial feminism

This book has not been organized as per national and geopolitical boundaries to enable the fluidity of geographies, identities, and phenomena to travel across borders. I was mindful of the risk of geographic oversimplification because, for example, one chapter deals with both India and Pakistan; likewise, one of the authors is of Indian origin but has written a co-authored chapter in the context of Pakistan. Further, many of the contributing authors do not live in India, Pakistan, or Bangladesh; however, their country of origin/biological roots and positionalities as researchers are anchored in those contexts. One author has written about a phenomenon in the context of Bangladesh but has imported evidence from the context of India. These instances remind us to be attentive to the borders and histories and imagine the (non)fluidity of borders, ideas, identities, or phenomena.

Each chapter uniquely concretizes postcolonial feminism, focusing on the different focal local phenomena, yet unified in their theoretical intentions of decolonizing the dominant Western knowledge in the organization studies.

Part 1 comprises two chapters. Chapter 2, "Naila Kabeer: Deconstructing empowerment of poor women entrepreneurs in postcolonial Bangladesh" by Afreen Huq, draws on the work of Naila Kabeer to engage in a feminist resistance to the subalternity of Bangladeshi women as "poor" and critique the idea of "development" in the postcolonial context of Bangladesh. Chapter 3, "The continued silencing of Gayatri Spivak's subaltern: A critique of the elite nexus of NGOs, academia, and corporations" by Rashed Chowdhury and Farooq Ahmad, exposes the exploitation of the subaltern position of poor rural farmers by the large capitalistic multinational corporation in the name of "social responsibility." They theorize this phenomenon, using the work of Gayatri Spivak, especially, her idea of "subalternity" ("can subaltern speak?"). In doing so, the authors expose the neo-colonial relations in the post-colonies that reproduce the colonial past. Both the chapters urge for the decolonization of MOS wherein the idea of "development" and "corporate social responsibility" are studied either in an ahistorical manner or as an all-good/positive phenomenon toward emancipation of the poor in the developing nations. Both chapters show that approaching a

MOS phenomenon through postcolonial feminism illuminates the underlying tensions in more nuanced and local ways.

Part II comprises two chapters. Chapter 4, "Colonialism otherwise: Reading Uzma Falak's Kashmir" by Ayesha Masood and Sadhvi Dar, shows how the neo-colonial relations between historically colonized ironically make those occupied as colonizers of each other. The authors draw on the work of the Kashmiri poet, filmmaker, and essayist, Uzma Falak to frame a decolonial feminist approach to theorizing the experiences of Kashmiri women. The chapter highlights how India and Pakistan, both postcolonial states, took colonizer's positions on the issue of Kashmir at different points in time. It has an important implication as it indicates that neo-colonial structures can emerge from within and between previously colonized units in new ways. Chapter 5, "Modern slavery in contemporary India: Addressing the elephant in the room – Contributions from Stringer and Samonova" by Swati Nagar, elaborates how modern slavery in the form of bonded and forced labor and human trafficking has assumed a neo-colonial arrangement of exploitation of women in India's patriarchal and post-colonial society. She shows how modern slavery is colonial, gendered, and reinforces class and caste demarcations. She also expresses concern about the paucity of academic and pedagogical literature in business schools on modern slavery in India.

Part III in this book represents two chapters that speak of and speak to management education and praxis in the post-colonies of India and Pakistan. Chapter 6, "The epistemology of the toilet: Doing class work in Pakistan" by Gazhal Zulfiqar and Ajnesh Prasad, uncovers the postcolonial feminist issues such as class and caste-inequalities and elitism among the B-school future managers vis-à-vis the toilet cleaners in the context of the post-colony of Pakistan as well as the importance of courses with postcolonial feminist lenses in the management development programs of elite management schools in India. Chapter 7, "Bringing postcolonial women writers to executive education: Case of women managers' program in India" by Nimruji Jammulamadaka and Padmavati Akella, discusses how women executive programs incorporating reflexive exercises that address the marginalized issues of gender and postcoloniality raise awareness among the female executive participants. The authors critique the dominant West-influenced management education, including executive education, in India that obscures the local challenges of patriarchy and postcolonialism, in the praxis of management. The authors urge more relevant and inclusive courses and course material toward the decolonization of management education and praxis.

The women writers and poets focused on in this book are those whose work the contributing chapter authors deemed valuable in illuminating the local postcolonial feminist issues in the contexts of India, Pakistan, and Bangladesh. This book does not intend to be an exhaustive coverage of women writers who have worked in the field of postcolonial feminism. Besides those covered in this book, there are many influential or under-recognized women writers that future research should focus on. We hope this book ignites the interest and zeal among the MOS students, scholars, and practitioners to carry forward the conversation initiated in this book and include not only different contexts from the Global South but also various women whose work may inform and advance the field of postcolonial feminism.

Notes

1. It is beyond the scope of this chapter and book to elaborate on the works that separately constitute feminism or postcolonialism.
2. Imperialism means exercising control over others through non-traditional means such as economic and political power and not necessarily traditional physical territorial conquest like colonialism (Prasad, 2003).
3. I am aware that "First-World feminism" or "western feminism" is not monolithic either and not acknowledging this would mean building yet another imperialist discourse that one is wanting to challenge.

Recommended Readings

Falak, U. (2016). For Mnemosyne. Two poems. *Himal Southasian.* www.himalmag. com/for-mnemosyne/.

Jammulamadaka, N. (2019). *Workers and margins: Grasping erasures and opportunities.* Palgrave Macmillan. https://doi.org/10.1007/978-981-13-7876-8

Kabeer, N. (2008). *Mainstreaming gender and social protection in the informal economy.* Commonwealth Secretariat.

Samonova, E. (2019). *Modern slavery and bonded labour in South Asia – A human rights-based approach.* Routledge.

Spivak, G. C. (1988). Can the subaltern speak? In C. Nelson & L. Grossberg (Eds.), *Marxism and the interpretation of culture* (pp. 271–313). University of Illinois Press.

Spivak, G. C. (1998). *In other worlds: Essays in cultural politics.* Routledge.

Zulfiqar, G., & Prasad, A. (2021). Challenging social inequality in the Global South: Class, privilege, and consciousness-raising through critical management education. *Academy of Management Learning and Education, 20*(2), 156–181.

References

Banerjee, S. B., & Jackson, L. (2017). Microfinance and the business of poverty reduction: Critical perspectives from rural Bangladesh. *Human Relations, 70*(1), 63–91.

Banerjee, S. B., & Linstead, S. (2004). Masking subversion: Neocolonial embeddedness in anthropological accounts of indigenous management. *Human Relations, 57*(2), 221–247.

Banerjee, B. S., & Prasad, A. (2008). Introduction to the special issue on "Critical reflections on management and organizations: A postcolonial perspective". *Critical Perspectives on International Business, 4*(2/3), 90–98.

Bell, E., Merilainen, S., Taylor, S., & Tienari, J. (2019). Time's up! Feminist theory and activism meets organization studies. *Human Relations, 72*(1), 4–22.

Calás, M. B., & Smircich, L. (1996). From 'the woman's' point of view': Feminist approaches to organization studies. In S. R. Clegg, C. Hardy, & W. L. Nord (Eds.), *Handbook of organization studies* (pp. 218–57). Sage Publications.

Crane, A., Soundararajan, V., Bloomfield, M., LeBaron, G., & Spence, L. J. (2022). Hybrid (un)freedom in worker hostels in garment supply chains. *Human Relations, 75*(10), https://doi.org/10.1177/00187267221081

Doshi, V. (2020). Symbolic violence in embodying customer service work across the urban/rural divide. *Gender, Work & Organization, 28*(1), 39–53.

Doshi, V. (2022). Experiencing liminality: At the crossroads of neoliberal and gendered experiences. *Gender, Work & Organization, 29*(4), 1132–1148.

Fanon, F. (2008). *Black skin, white masks*. Pluto.

Gandhi, L. (1998). *Postcolonial theory: A critical introduction*. Oxford University Press.

Harding, N., Ford, J., & Fotaki, M. (2012). Is the 'F'-word still dirty? A past, present, and future of/for feminist and gender studies in organization. *Organization, 20*(1), 51–65.

Jack, G., Westwood, R., Srinivas, N., et al. (2011). Deepening, broadening and re-asserting a postcolonial interrogative space in organization studies. *Organization, 18*(3), 275–302.

Jones, C. (2005). Practical deconstructivist feminist Marxist organization theory: Gayatri Chakravorty Spivak. *The Sociological Review, 53*(1), 228–244.

Lewis, R., & Mills, S. (Eds.). (2003). *Feminist postcolonial theory: A reader*. Routledge.

Liddle, J., & Joshi, R. (1985). Gender and imperialism in British India. *Economic and Political Weekly, 20*(43), WS72–WS78.

Lugones, M. (2010). Toward a decolonial feminism. *Hypatia, 25*(4), 742–759.

Manning, J. (2021). Decolonial feminist theory: Embracing the gendered colonial difference in management and organisation studies. *Gender, Work & Organization, 28*, 1203–1219.

Min-ha, T. (1989). *Woman, native, other: Writing postcoloniality and feminism*. Indiana University Press.

Mignolo, W. D. (2011). Geopolitics of sensing and knowing: On (de) coloniality, border thinking, and epistemic disobedience. *Postcolonial Studies, 14*(3), 273–283.

Mohanty, C. T. (1988). Under Western eyes: Feminist scholarship and colonial discourses. *Feminist Review, 30*, 61–88.

Mohanty, C. T. (2003a). 'Under Western eyes' revisited: Feminist solidarity through anticapitalist struggles. *Signs: Journal of Women in Culture and Society, 28*(2), 499–535.

Mohanty, C. T. (2003b). *Feminism without borders: Decolonizing theory, practicing solidarity*. Duke University Press.

Mooten, N. (2015). *Toward a postcolonial ethics of care: In what interest, to regulate what sort of relationships, is the globe evoked? Gayatri Spivak.* Retrieved March 15, 2022, from https://ethicsofcare.org/wp-content/uploads/2016/12/Toward_a_Postcolonial_Ethics_of_Care.pdf

Munir, K., Ayaz, M., Levy, D. L., & Willmott, H. (2018). The role of intermediaries in governance of global production networks: Restructuring work relations in Pakistan's apparel industry. *Human Relations, 71*(4), 560–583.

Narayan, U. (2004). The project of feminist epistemology: Perspectives from a non-Western feminist. *The Feminist Standpoint Theory Reader: Intellectual and Political Controversies,* 213–224.

Narayan, U. (2019). Sisterhood and "doing good": Asymmetries of Western feminist location, access and orbits of concern. *Feminist Philosophy Quarterly, 5*(2), https://doi.org/10.5206/fpq/2019.2.7299

Nkomo, S. M. (2011). A postcolonial and anti-colonial reading of 'African' leadership and management in organization studies: Tensions, contradictions and possibilities. *Organization, 18*(3), 365–386.

Özkazanç-Pan, B. (2012). Postcolonial feminist research: Challenges and complexities. *Equality, Diversity and Inclusion: An International Journal, 31*(5), 573–591.

Prasad, A. (2003). *Postcolonial theory and organizational analysis.* Palgrave Macmillan.

Spivak, G. C. (1981). French feminism in an international frame. *Yale French Studies, 62,* 154–184.

Spivak, G. C. (1988). Can the subaltern speak? In C. Nelson & L. Grossberg (Eds.), *Marxism and the interpretation of culture* (pp. 271–313). University of Illinois Press.

Spivak, G. C. (1990). In S. Harasym (Ed.), *The post-colonial critic: Interviews, strategies, dialogues with Gayatri Chakravorty Spivak.* Routledge.

Suleri, S. (1992). Woman skin deep: Feminism and the postcolonial condition. *Critical Inquiry, 18*(4), 756–769.

Part I

Feminist Resistance to Subalternity

Deconstructing "Development" and "Social Responsibility"

2 Naila Kabeer

Deconstructing Empowerment of Poor Women Entrepreneurs in Postcolonial Bangladesh

Afreen Huq

Introduction

This chapter discusses the entrepreneurial discourse of empowerment in the context of the conditions faced by poor Bangladeshi women engaged in home-based work and micro-enterprises in a postcolonial political environment. It draws on the writings of feminist scholar Naila Kabeer, looking to synthesize and build on major findings in her prolific work in the area, with the aid of complementary research from other scholars and my own empirical work. To that end, this chapter focuses in particular on the concept of "agency" as it features in Kabeer's conceptualization of empowerment.

Kabeer has discussed the importance for poor women in Bangladesh (homeworkers and micro-entrepreneurs) to exercise strategic forms of personal agency concerning their own private lives; the same is true of strategic forms of collective agency in relation to larger structures of constraint that subordinate them to men (Kabeer, 1999, 2001, 2016; Gammage et al., 2016). It is the latter emphasis in Kabeer's work that merits closer examination, this chapter contends; they must be drawn out in light of their critical import for the key issue of empowerment.

Crucially, Kabeer contends that entrepreneurial discourse loses its meaning as a form of empowerment (1) without social and historical context and (2) without collective action. As we will see, this becomes particularly important in light of Bangladesh's social developments in the period since Independence, in terms of both ongoing attacks on women's rights and the formation of women's movements in self-defense. These developments are at least partly reflected in development discourse, where "poor Bangladeshi women" tend to be portrayed as passive and powerless, but for the intervention of westerners; poverty reduction means women's economic empowerment in this context (Shikdar, 2003).

Agency, Kabeer argues, is not so much an outcome of increases in available income, but rather "is associated with an apparent transformation in

DOI: 10.4324/9781003197270-3

values and attitudes in the larger society" (2016, p. 313). Empowerment, therefore, functions as opportunities for women to exercise their agency and shift unequal power relations (Kabeer, 2016). Consciousness, voice, and action are all facets of agency, encompassing both the individual and collective exercise of agency (Grammage et al., 2016). I include my own empirical research on women's entrepreneurship and empowerment outcomes for women in Bangladesh to situate and ground the arguments in the local context. Connecting language to what socially situated individuals do both at the broader level of culture and in specific situations (Lillis, 2001; Vygotsky, 1978), my synthesis of Kabeer's writings links to my cultural world views drawn from my own personal life experiences as a Bangladeshi-born academic.

The analysis of power is central to contemporary development discourse. Much of this focus on power has its roots in postcolonial and feminist theories, which have had significant consequences for how development is conceptualized. Postcolonial approaches problematize the ways in which the world is known, challenging the unacknowledged assumptions at the heart of Western disciplines; such are profoundly insensitive to the meanings, values, and practices of other cultures. They challenge the meaning of development, rooted in colonial discourse, depicting the North as advanced and progressive and the South as backward, degenerate, and primitive.

Building on this analysis, I discuss in the chapter to follow the link between Bangladeshi women, entrepreneurial discourse of empowerment, and postcolonial context/discourse as they relate to Kabeer's concept of agency. I focus on the latter in light of the social context of "postcolonial" Bangladesh, and traditional forms of entrepreneurialism as a strategy of economic development. I explore the meaning of agency as Kabeer develops it for poor women entrepreneurs and the meaning as applied within inherently colonial discourses of development, considering the prospects for empowerment considering tensions between the two and related issues of collective empowerment and the constraints associated with class and patriarchal hierarchies.

Kabeer's Concept of Agency

Kabeer (1999) mentions that empowerment can be best understood in terms of the process by which women, traditionally denied the ability to make strategic life choices, can acquire that ability. The process by which this occurs, notes Kabeer, involves three interrelated dimensions: resources, agency, and achievements. Resources include not only access, but also future claims, to both material and human and social resources; agency includes processes of decision-making, as well as less measurable manifestations of agency like negotiation, deception, and manipulation; achievements include well-being outcomes (Kabeer, 1999, p. 435, 2005, p. 14).

Kabeer draws a distinction between "passive" forms of agency (action taken when there is little choice), and "active" agency (purposeful behavior), and a further distinction between greater "effectiveness" of agency, and "transformative" agency (Kabeer, 2005, p. 15). She stresses the importance of transformative forms of agency that do not simply address immediate inequalities, but also initiate longer-term processes of change in the structures of patriarchy. While changes in the consciousness and agency of individual women are an important starting point for such processes, it will do little on its own to address the systemic reproduction of inequality (Kabeer, 2005, pp. 15–24).

In discussing resources, agency, and achievements, Kabeer contends for successfully linking power and choice, as long as what is chosen contributes to the welfare of those making the choice. This is significant insofar as forms of gender inequality are much harder to overcome when normalized by the victims (Kabeer, 1999). Women undermine their own well-being by capitulating to their husbands' primary claims on household resources and their violence, or through their preparedness to risk their own health and survival to bear sons (Kabeer, 1999). This reminds us, Kabeer says, that power relations and dominance can operate through consent and complicity as well as through coercion and conflict.

Meaningful empowerment strategies, then, must avoid the "highly qualified notion of choice" that rationalizes the subordinate status of women, and the internalization of these values by women themselves. In focusing on the social context of gender relations, advocates of gender and social justice must be sensitive to how power relations shape – indeed, distort – processes of empowerment (Kabeer, 1999). As a practical example, Kabeer cites the third Millennium Development Goal (MDG) relies on indicators of progress – closing the gender gap in education, increasing women's share of wage employment in the non-agricultural sector, and increasing the proportion of seats held by women in national parliaments. While certainly worthy, these metrics nevertheless neglect to treat the underlying hierarchical and patriarchal social relationships that govern access to such resources (Kabeer, 2005).

The concept of women's empowerment, Kabeer continues, was once the domain of grassroots women's organizations in developing countries. Its adoption by a diverse range of actors, including microfinance organizations, has given rise to definitions that have gradually neutralized its original political edge (Kabeer, 2017). What is missing in previous studies, Kabeer contends, is attention to women's ability to exercise agency in wider aspects of their lives, particularly their status as citizens and their ability to challenge social injustice. At the same time, she argues, we must also attend to forms of change that have consequences for the wider structures of inequality in society, as well as for individual women.

While structural change may come about as the unintended consequences of aggregated individual actions, our interest here is on more purposive efforts to bring it about (Kabeer, 2017). Gender equality is an intrinsic rather than an instrumentalist goal, an end, rather than a means of achieving other goals (Kabeer, 2005).

Limitations of the "Postcolonial" Bangladesh

Post-coloniality is critical to understanding empowerment insofar as it highlights the ongoing social role of gender and class hierarchy. Understanding the role such hierarchies play in shaping (and distorting) empowerment processes, in turn, demands social and historical context. Key to this understanding is the rise of state-sponsored religious fundamentalism in South Asia signaling a marked shift away from equal rights discourse. Coupled with attacks on legal and political rights women had already won, these developments reflect ruling class efforts to manage the breakdown of traditionally patriarchal social structures, and the crisis of political legitimacy that results for themselves (Chhachhi, 1989). Ruling parties promote socially regressive policies that privilege males within caste and class hierarchies, trading away the rights of women for the loyalty of male subjects to an authoritarian, top-down political unity predicated on submission to fundamentalist values and doctrine (Chhachhi, 1989).

In lieu of addressing the root causes for which they are responsible, Chhachhi (1989) states, ruling parties seek a political unity built on religious sectarianism. This "communalism" is an essentially tribal approach that suppresses caste, gender, and class tensions and generates an "Other" for the purposes of blame-shifting and blaming of the victim (Debney, 2020). The outcome is a tribal or "communal identity" that, Chhachhi surmises, "has no natural basis but has to be created." The resulting "false consciousness" reinforces the unspoken assumption that the interests of ruling and subordinate classes are identical (Chhachhi, 1989, pp. 568–570). Having a precedent in the colonial period, when it presented a significant strategy for thwarting the movement for independent nationalism, communalism rooted in religion offered a "safety valve" amidst, again, "a challenge to and breakdown of traditional patriarchal structures and the process of identity creation in situations of social and economic crisis" (Chhachhi, 1989, p. 571).

One result of these developments is the continued prevalence of the "woman question" in the public sphere, even within postcolonial society.

While the patriarchal status quo regards women as productive bodies, gender norms regarding reproductive responsibilities remain uncontested (Siddiqi & Ashraf, 2017). During a period of growth between 1995 and 2003, export-oriented production in South Asia expanded exponentially. Women and girls flooding into Dhaka and Chittagong were compelled to "adapt and accommodate" to, rather than challenge, gender-dominant social norms, given the "authoritarian and hierarchical nature of the private sector. The increased number of married mothers in the labor force led to a moral crisis for working women, required now to 'balance' cultural expectations as good carers with their professional obligations" (Siddiqi & Ashraf, 2017, pp. 123–126).

Societal expectations that women must be carers first, and workers second has a distinct class dimension (Siddiqi & Ashraf, 2017, p. 126). Professionals can rely on privatized systems of care – a fact that simply reproduces class privilege. Managerial practices put the productive worker and the "good" (docile) woman who prioritizes unpaid, domestic care labor on a pedestal, while demonizing the "disreputable" labor organizer and devaluing the work of women as breadwinners (Siddiqi & Ashraf, 2017, p. 127). Women workers are expected to fit in domestic social reproduction around formal work; they must juggle social pressure to earn and be productive, and patriarchal norms tying them to unpaid care labor (Siddiqi & Ashraf, 2017).

NGOs looking to microcredit and market-based success as a way for working women to enhance their ability to care for their families reflects the cultural logic that thrusts the moral imperative onto them to take responsibility for their household. This class blindness reflects a failure by the feminist movement to rethink broader institutional arrangements – not least of which is redressing the systemic nature of gendered inequalities and the precarity of available employment (Siddiqi & Ashraf, 2017).

For Kabeer, this is a critical facet of history insofar as Bangladeshi state planners implicitly subsumed women's interests under the interests of the population, assuming that economic benefits would eventually trickle down to them. She quotes a US – AID economist acknowledging with the wisdom of hindsight,

> I admit to an early misconception that the female half of the population naturally benefits from overall growth. I now recognize a few of the problems that a male-dominated society causes and the economic advantages to be gained from female participation in achieving developmental objectives.
>
> (Kabeer, 1988, p. 98)

Even a cursory glance at what has been achieved in the nearly two decades since Bangladesh gained its independence, Kabeer concludes, is sufficient to reveal the hollowness of the promises the Bangladesh ruling class made in the heady aftermath of liberation, the promises of a state built on the principles of secularism, democracy, nationalism, and socialism. The patriarchal family system in Bangladesh is looking increasingly shaky; it is now apparent that its ability to contain large numbers of women within material and social dependency can no longer be guaranteed (Kabeer, 1988).

These observations gain greater currency because Kabeer and Chhachhi published their respective articles three decades ago. Many of the emerging tendencies appear to have been realized in contemporary Hindu nationalism, indicating the ongoing value of communalism and fundamentalist tribalism for South Asian elites, and so something of the root causes of the patriarchal structures continuing to frustrate women's empowerment.

Development in a Context of Structural Inequality

With historical context for the role class and gender hierarchies play in shaping (and distorting) empowerment approaches, Kabeer (2020) explores the economic thinking through which the power relations associated with them are asserted, focusing on the conflict between structural inequality and approaches to development emphasizing individual choices. While many are concerned that economic dependency is a major factor in structuring inequalities, Kabeer (1997, p. 261) notes that jobs generated by export opportunities are frequently exploitative and do little to address women's economic dependency; feminist scholars thus remain agnostic about the emancipatory potential of such employment in general.

The thinking associated with these developments was exemplified, Kabeer surmises, by the randomized control trials (RCTs) for which three scholars were awarded the 2019 Nobel Prize in economics. Despite claims of impartiality, Kabeer mentions, the *randomista* method and narrative are not objective or impartial but ignore what feminists have long espoused: that the formation of preferences derives from entrenched social constructions. This is reflected in the guiding assumption of the *randomistas* that, while gender equality is desirable in its own right, it is better achieved through gender-neutral policies, because gender-affirmative policies "distort" the allocative process, leading to efficiency costs (Kabeer, 2020, p. 1).

These so-called distortions, Kabeer notes, stem however from historical structures that have curtailed women's productive potential, protecting male privilege. Patriarchal discrimination introduces structural costs unlikely to be visible when the focus is on individual economic actors. The *randomista* argument has not been borne out by recent data revealing that patriarchal discrimination introduces structural costs unlikely to be visible when the focus is on individual economic actors (Kabeer, 2020). As data collected by the World Economic Forum suggests, economic growth has not been accompanied by progress on gender equality, either economically or politically (Kabeer, 2020).

Indeed, as Kabeer (2017) notes elsewhere, denial of economic resources to women, and their resulting lifelong dependency on men, has long been foundational to their subordinate status throughout Bangladesh. While empowerment entails change in the lives of individual women and their interpersonal relations, active citizenship remains the basis for women's capacity to participate in the public life of their community (Kabeer, 2017, p. 649). Most quantitative studies of women's empowerment carried out in Bangladesh, fail to adequately establish whether, for instance, evidence of an empirical association between paid work and women's empowerment reflects the empowerment potential of the activity in question, or the fact that empowered women are more likely to take up such activity (Kabeer, 2017, p. 649). Kabeer concludes that women's access to income-earning opportunities is important, but that neither involvement with microfinance nor women's income-earning capacity has much influence on more coercive aspects of family relationships, like appropriation of women's valued possessions and restrictions on their ability to work outside the home (Kabeer, 2017, p. 660).

As means of implementing these strategies, Kabeer notes that empowerment advocates have had success by building on "claimed synergies" between feminist goals and official development priorities – though the translation of feminist insights into policy discourse has also led to "fuzziness" (Kabeer, 1999, pp. 435–436). For Kabeer, however, the meaning of empowerment is clear insofar as poverty and disempowerment are clearly connected; insufficient means for meeting basic needs preclude the ability to exercise meaningful choice. Meaningful empowerment should thus increase the ability to make strategic life choices where this ability was previously denied (Kabeer, 1999).

Dolan et al. (2012, p. 34) contextualize Kabeer's observations by exploring the emergence of "market-based" approaches to development, noting the increasing tendency for large corporations to embrace women's empowerment as their "cause." Whether such schemes provide a model for broad-based, sustainable development, the authors note, remains inconclusive; little consensus exists on how to determine whether entrepreneurial activity is empowering (Dolan et al., 2012, p. 38). In a country where only four per cent of women aged 20–55 earn a cash income, only one-third have completed primary school, and only a tenth junior secondary school, Dolan et al. (2012, pp. 35–39) conclude that participation in the CARE

Bangladesh Rural Sales Programme (RSP) has enhanced women's capacity to exercise agency in their personal and familial lives with positive outcomes. At the same time, they found less evidence that it leads to collective empowerment or the capacity to effect broad-based social and political change (Dolan et al., 2012).

Similarly, Heintz et al. (2018) note a considerable body of evidence from Bangladesh pointing to the positive impacts of paid work on women's position within family and community. According to official statistics, however, women's labor force participation has risen only slowly over the years, while unpaid family labor also continues to feature for a sizeable majority of women in the labor force (Heintz et al., 2018, p. 266). The steady growth of microfinance services specifically targeting women and the emergence of new opportunities for home-based income-generating activity, Heintz et al. (2018, p. 286) add, reinforces the tendency to opt for work within the home.

The primary appeal of microfinance for women, the authors note, is its compatibility with *purdah* (meaning curtain, is the word used to describe the system of secluding women and enforcing high standards of female modesty) norms; the spread of microfinance in Bangladesh has effectively served to subsidize the withdrawal from wage labor by some women and to reinforce the decision on the part of others to opt for home-based work. Progress in terms of women's engagement in the economy overall, however, remains slow (Heintz et al., 2018).

Patriarchal Bargains in Colonial Development Discourse

Delving deeper into the distortion of the popular women's movement for empowerment, Kabeer (1997) examines the implications of women's access to wage labor for their position in intra-household relationships, considering the extent to which this reflects a "patriarchal bargain." Within Bangladeshi households, bargaining power is not equally distributed, but reflects the relative strength of members fallback positions – the potential utilities they would enjoy should household cooperation collapse. The implications for questions of gender and class power are clear; the person who is going to "end up in more of a mess" is less well-equipped to secure favorable bargaining outcomes; the threat or use of violence factors in determining breakdown positions (Kabeer, 1997, p. 263).

The concrete constraints generated by these rules shape the terms of the "patriarchal bargain" and its potential for active or passive resistance to male power. The translation of women's earning power into greater bargaining power within the household will reflect the perceived costs to women of seeking to re-negotiate the terms of the pre-existing "patriarchal bargain" (Kabeer, 1997, p. 266). Power relations manifest then, not so much through observable conflicts in decision-making, but rather through deeply entrenched cultural norms and values that systematically privilege certain household members over others and tend to be taken for granted by all members of the household (Kabeer, 1997).

For Bangladeshi women, Kabeer (2011, p. 500) adds, this reflects "path dependency" insofar as women's subordinate status is a product of prevailing patriarchal structures of constraint in Bangladeshi society. Processes of empowerment occur, in other words, occur within specific contexts and are shaped by them – in particular, by prevailing gender-related structures of constraint. Since these structures influence the pace, substance, and direction of social change, as well as defining areas of "inertness," empowerment pathways are generally characterized by path dependence. They carry the imprint of the societies in which they occur (Kabeer, 2011).

Kabeer (2011, p. 500) finds little evidence to suggest that these changes have enabled women from poor rural households to articulate and act on their vision of social justice. The overall consequences of these interacting constraints, she surmises, mean that not only is women's access to material resources extremely limited, but their social interactions are restricted to the "given" relations of family and kinship, rendering them dependent on male family members.

This marked dependence on men for economic needs and social protection leaves women particularly vulnerable to "patriarchal risk" – the likelihood, in other words, of abrupt declines in their economic welfare and social status should they find themselves bereft of male guardianship (Kabeer, 2011, p. 501). However, it is not only the strength of their material stake in the system that has kept women locked into a subordinate position. Strong ideological factors are also at play (Kabeer, 2011).

If injustices are ingrained in the social relationships that construct women's sense of self and security within their communities, Kabeer notes, they are also likely to be ingrained in women's gendered subjectivities (Kabeer, 2011, p. 503). Considering conceptualizing the household as a cooperative venture run by a benevolent dictator in the interests of all is clearly not satisfactory, insofar as this alleges altruism and choice when clear evidence exists of the various overt, covert, and sometimes violent ways in which men exercise power over women domestically (Kabeer, 1997, p. 300).

Conflicts in Domestic and Social Power

In the context of development discourses where the legitimacy of the patriarchal bargain is taken for granted, Kabeer (2010) argues, worldviews that underlie development interventions are likely to be biased against those who exercise little voice in either the formulation of these theories or their translation into interventions. In other words, development interventions do not always promote, or even seek to promote, greater justice in society (Kabeer, 2010, pp. 105–106).

Gender is one of the most pervasive examples of social inequality: women's needs, interests, and experiences have been systematically excluded, misrepresented, or subsumed with those of men within development policy and planning (Kabeer, 2010, p. 106). Gender-specific norms and values tend then to be rooted informally (Kabeer, 2010, p. 107). Insofar as they break down the power of the "patriarchal bargain" and check the effectiveness of violence, factory wages, Kabeer finds, have helped to transform the parameters within which women workers make choices (Kabeer, 1997).

Kabeer et al. (2018, p. 236) note further that research into the empowerment potential of women's access to labor market opportunities – one that has taken on fresh lease of life in the Bangladesh context with the increased feminization of paid work amidst economic liberalization – has not been able to address these questions in using very narrow definitions of work and of empowerment.

Collective Action and Empowerment

The systemic nature of patriarchy, Kabeer et al. (2018, p. 237) contend, suggests that solutions to problems of women's vulnerability and lack of income-earning opportunities will not be easily reached. While paid work can act as a pathway to change beyond the economic domain, they also find that access to paid work had greater impact at the individual and familial level than at that of the community. Few women voted in both national and local elections, far fewer voted according to their own conscience. Even fewer had taken part in election campaigns, participated in village decision-making forums, or engaged in collective action to protest injustice or claim their rights. Individual empowerment through education and work, in other words, had not translated into greater voice within the community, or collective efforts to challenge gender injustice (Kabeer et al., 2018, p. 250).

While the universal value that many feminists claim for individual autonomy, Kabeer (2011, p. 500) elaborates, may not therefore have the same purchase in all contexts, it is through their mutual interactions that the empowerment of individual women is most likely to translate into broader struggles for gender justice and social transformation. This fact reflects the importance of social relationships in the construction of identity and consciousness: The "I" becomes an "I" only among a "we" in a community of speech and action (Kabeer, 2011, p. 503).

Grammage et al. (2016) develop these arguments by examining and analyzing evolving definitions of voice and agency. Structure and agency are closely intertwined with manifestations of power; structures shape the agency of individuals and groups, but individual and collective agency can also reproduce, modify, or transform structures (Gammage et al., 2016, p. 1). The authors refer approvingly on this count to Sen's work on cooperative conflict, which, as they note, highlights how inequalities of power can manifest as silence and apparent consent to the existing arrangements if oppressive structures lead to "adapted preferences," or adaptation by oppressed groups to the status quo.

Sen's writing was of particular interest to the question of empowerment, Gammage et al. (2016, p. 3) reveal, insofar as drawing attention to the role of ideology in systematically devaluing the work of women within the household hierarchy – with significant implications where approaches to women's empowerment relied for proof on subjective testimony from those concerned. Gammage et al. (2016, p. 4) note relevant contributions from Agarwal, whose research on household bargaining they consider as breaking new ground in drawing explicit attention to the role of norms in both their constraining and enabling forms; struggles over resources manifest within the intimate domain of the family.

Such innovations in research, Gammage et al. (2016, pp. 4–5) suggest, help to illustrate the kinds of agency that subordinate groups can bring to bear when they have intimate knowledge of those wielding authority over them – also draws attention to broader institutional influences on its realization. This, the authors claim, is particularly significant in terms of its bearing on collective action by women cooperating in various organizational forms – from cooperatives and political parties to social movements, women's organizations, trade unions, and user groups. In going well beyond individual agency, such examples, they note, reflect the potential of collective action to enable women to challenge, transform, and overcome gendered structures of constraint (Gammage et al., 2016, p. 5).

It is here that the significance of "evolving politics of claims-making" by women workers in the global South becomes more apparent. For women in the global South seeking justice at the national level, by contrast, organizations of women workers tend, often with the support of locally-based NGOs, to be the source of claims, reflecting the value to these workers of self-activity and collective action (Kabeer, 2015, p. 1). This is particularly pertinent when it comes to global value chains (Kabeer, 2015).

Women workers, Kabeer notes, have organized in forms as varied as trade unions, associations, and cooperatives – sometimes opting to work along the union movement, sometimes opting to set up independent organizations.

Either way, autonomy and organizational spaces that allow for it are critical for women workers in pursuing gender and economic justice (Kabeer, 2015, p. 2).

Decolonizing Pathways of Empowerment

Tying together her discussion of the conditions that the struggle for women's empowerment meets in the context of nominally postcolonial Bangladesh, Kabeer (2016) reviews the long-standing preoccupation with economic growth in international policy circles. She finds that evidence that gender equality contributed positively to economic growth to be fairly robust, noting that growth modelling in neoclassical economics confines itself to a few measures of gender equality: education, employment, and sometimes wages. Efforts to model gender equality, on the other hand, are relatively new, drawing on a wider range of equality measures, including well-being, rights, and political participation (Kabeer, 2016, p. 296).

Kabeer also finds that these macro-level studies provide few insights into what these pathways might be. Feminists agree with neoclassical economists that individuals make choices and exercise agency within the limits imposed by their personal circumstances, but also draw attention to the constraints posed by rules, norms, resources, and identities between different groups, along lines of gender, class, race, and caste, and the inequalities of power and privilege these generate (Kabeer, 2016). In Bangladesh, cultural expectations of women's dependency mean these regions experienced the phenomenon of "missing women" (Kabeer, 2016, p. 298). This has led feminist scholars to argue that a key criterion for assessing the gender implications of growth strategies must be their capacity to address the consequences of structural constraints (Kabeer, 2016, p. 299).

In light of the resilience of certain aspects of patriarchy, Kabeer mentions, gender equality should be made on intrinsic rather than instrumental grounds; the evidence in support of the instrumental argument, she notes, relies strongly on women's conformity to socially ascribed maternal roles. This constrains their ability to participate in economic activity on equal terms with men, and to participate more generally in the public life of their community (Kabeer, 2016, p. 316). Kabeer is more convinced by contemporary evidence highlighting the importance of women's collective agency. Collective action by women has, as we have seen, proven to be the single most important driving force in promoting women's rights (Kabeer, 2016, pp. 316–317).

Other research supports these conclusions. McEwan (2001) proposes that an analysis of power, with a view to producing a "truly decolonized, postcolonial knowledge," is central to contemporary development studies

(McEwan, 2001, p. 93). The dominant "development" discourse remains unconsciously ethnocentric, rooted in European cultures and reflecting a domineering Western world-view; unacknowledged assumptions at its core are rooted in colonial discourse, depicting the North as advanced and progressive and the South as backward, degenerate and primitive (McEwan, 2001, p. 94). The term "the Third World" itself homogenizes people and countries, carrying connotations of economic backwardness and developmental failure underwritten by a binary contest between "self" and "other" (McEwan, 2001, p. 95).

All of this serves to demonstrate, McEwan (2001, p. 95) states, that the Western idea of development has enabled the west to appropriate and control the non-west. The historical and contemporary voices of the marginalized, oppressed, and dominated are lost, the notion of a single path to development reigns supreme, and peoples of the Third World are represented as passive, helpless victims (McEwan, 2001, pp. 95–96). A product of Western cultural politics, Western feminism reflects Western understandings of sexual politics and gender relations, such that many women in the global South associate it with cultural imperialism (McEwan, 2001). For them, gender oppression is inextricably bound up with "race" and class (McEwan, 2001).

Postcolonial feminisms seek, then, to contest the Western emphasis on "discourse," which detracts from the reality of persistent colonial power relations; the power dynamics and social relations of global capitalism are conspicuously absent (McEwan, 2001, pp. 101–102). In coming to terms with the consequences and interrelations of different sites of oppression: class, race, nation, and sexuality and recognizing the partial and situated quality of knowledge claims, Western feminists must avoid the "colonizing move" (McEwan, 2001, p. 106).

Kabeer and Huq (2010) address the question of the "colonizing move; by exploring social relationships in women's lives and their relationship to empowerment through collective action; such they contrast with the traditional social structures that limit Bangladeshi women's social interaction to their immediate family and maintain patriarchal controls." Community organizations based on collective action, Kabeer and Huq note, engendered bonds of friendship and loyalty between participants by facilitating relationships beyond the private sphere. Participants were more aware of their rights and local politics, more likely to demonstrate leadership skills, more likely to participate in local politics, and more likely to engage in collective action. Such reflected the significance of social relationships in women's lives and their relevance to processes of women's empowerment (Kabeer & Huq, 2010, p. 79).

While, traditionally, the analysis of efforts to bring about women's empowerment has rarely gone beyond "given" relationships in women's lives, Kabeer and Huq (2010) mention, evidence from Saptagram suggests that organizational strategies have implications for both the range and quality of relationships in women's lives. The groups women formed provided them with a form of organization that allowed them to define their interests for themselves, instead of having to accept socially determined priorities – an important break from the past (Kabeer & Huq, 2010, p. 81). They report that the women they had spoken to were by no means affluent but had achieved enough economic security to diminish their reliance on patronage relationships; they drew on the power of these social relationships in confronting hierarchies of domination within their community (Kabeer & Huq, 2010, p. 86).

Conclusion

From this synthesis of her work and its import, we surmise that Naila Kabeer has contributed to research into women's empowerment in South Asia mainly in the idea that the traditional approach to empowerment reflects a "colonizing move" not dissimilar to how Western feminists and development academics have approached women's rights issues in non-Western contexts. Just as development policies in South Asia reflect the needs of local elites and their transnational corporate patrons rather than those they affect, so do Western feminisms reflect the needs of Western feminists for interpretations of empowerment that sidesteps thorny issues of class and imperialism.

This symbiosis would seem to serve only to raise more questions about the relationship discussed earlier between policymakers in South Asian governments and empowerment advocates, especially if acceptance into a process far removed from grassroots community organizing and people power gives rise to compromises that hollow out the substance of empowerment while retaining forms for the sake of appearance.

It also inevitably leads back to the question of the meaning of empowerment in a "postcolonial" context. The continuing prevalence of "colonizing moves" suggests that colonialism has not ended, but merely changed form. Transnational corporations operating in South Asia, with the economic clout to capture national governments, assume the mantle formerly held by the colonial state. As Kabeer indicates, entrepreneurial discourses of gender in the postcolonial context become increasingly more fraught the more private corporate power assumes the mantle of colonial extractor, and the concept of empowerment is subsumed beneath them.

This helps account for the fact, as Delaney and Huq (2019) mention along with Kabeer, that despite the improvement in financial independence of home-based workers, it is less likely that the income they earn can translate into a more democratic distribution of intrahousehold power and meaningful exercise of agency. Having wages to spend might give home-based workers more freedom of mobility and self-worth than if they had none, but it is not the same as individual or collective agency as social actors. On this count, empowerment is not the same thing as empower-ment as initially conceived (Delaney & Huq, 2019). As the work of Kabeer reveals, empowerment is a collective concept and an approach that reflects the need for collective solutions to collective problems. This approach has produced a meaningful change in the past, and, as Kabeer's work demon-strates, is the safest bet for meaningful change in the future.

References

Chhachhi, A. (1989). The state, religious fundamentalism and women: Trends in South Asia, *Economic and Political Weekly*, *24*(11), 567–578. www.jstor.org/stable/4394529

Debney, B. M. (2020). *The oldest trick in the book: Panic-driven scapegoating in history and recurring patterns of persecution.* Palgrave.

Delaney, A., & Huq, A. (2019, February 12–14). *Challenging the entrepreneurial discourse around women home-based workers' empowerment.* Paper presented to The Association of Industrial Relations Academics in Australia and New Zealand (AIRAANZ) Conference.

Dolan, C., Johnstone-Louis, M., & Scott, L. (2012). Shampoo, saris and SIM cards: Seeking entrepreneurial futures at the bottom of the pyramid. *Gender & Development*, *20*(1), 33–47. https://doi.org/10.1080/13552074.2012.663619

Gammage, S., Kabeer, N., & Rodgers, Y. (2016). Voice and agency: Where are we now? *Feminist Economics*, *22*(1), 1–29. https://doi.org/10.1080/13545701.2015.1101308

Heintz, J., Kabeer, N., & Mahmud, S. (2018). Cultural norms, economic incentives and women's labor market behavior: Empirical insights from Bangladesh. *Oxford Development Studies*, *46*(2), 266–289. https://doi.org/10.1080/13600818.2017.1382464

Kabeer, N. (1988). Subordination and struggle: Women in Bangladesh. *New Left Review*, *168*(1), 95–121. https://newleftreview.org/issues/i168/articles/naila-kabeer-subordination-and-struggle-women-in-bangladesh.pdf

Kabeer, N. (1997). Women, wages and intra-household power relations in urban Bangladesh. *Development and Change*, *28*(2), 261–302. https://onlinelibrary.wiley.com/doi/pdf/10.1111/1467-7660.00043?casa_token=tJc3i-0198QAAAAA:DTQhNPwhxXW362oJoKwz50L-xC3D6D6Jmt0dlYzEdPRvI-2XqosqsUgS-hLwI0S9SV_sw0JmEner3PZYh

Kabeer, N. (1999). Resources, agency, achievements: Reflections on the measure-ment of women's empowerment. *Development and Change*, *30*(3), 435–464. https://onlinelibrary.wiley.com/doi/pdf/10.1111/1467-7660.00125?casa_token=STkDkXDyMBYAAAAA:OmXACMNUZDl-gtT7ccxfBnKTIzw6gGBW5ylE8LwRwLcjbDcRs1ggkpIW6jD8u950GepdYeT5jv1a0_fF

Kabeer, N. (2001). Conflicts over credit: Re-evaluating the empowerment potential of loans to women in rural Bangladesh. *World development*, *29*(1), 63–84.

Kabeer, N. (2005). Gender equality and women's empowerment: A critical analysis of the third millennium development goal 1. *Gender & Development*, *13*(1), 13–24. https://doi.org/10.1080/13552070512331332273

Kabeer, N. (2010). Women's empowerment, development interventions and the management of information flows. *ids Bulletin*, *41*(6), 105–113. https://onlinelibrary. wiley.com/doi/pdf/10.1111/j.1759-5436.2010.00188.x?casa_token=vcps4jegeO MAAAAA:JJbcY6Bo1W7pAuWoKwkf3c9KqGUGC7BfFKs4fX8hwshZu8ZX BOLx5iSvAWdTW8YeAD3epEY4SMcX580J

Kabeer, N. (2011). Between affiliation and autonomy: Navigating pathways of women's empowerment and gender justice in rural Bangladesh. *Development and Change*, *42*(2), 499–528. https://onlinelibrary.wiley.com/doi/pdf/10.1111/j.1467-7660.2011.01703.x?casa_token=0fxCghoRZ0UAAAAA:y79PFovBjYkuVOU KUwKG1FsUqb9F6RFpFQzhduyjq7nSNznE2ZuoUtmDFa2XCtZ5Cbxij7 3HvAMU4wpx

Kabeer, N. (2015). Women workers and the politics of claims-making in a globalizing economy (No. 2015–13). *UNRISD Working Paper*. www.econstor.eu/ bitstream/10419/148721/1/861089235.pdf

Kabeer, N. (2016). Gender equality, economic growth, and women's agency: The "endless variety" and "monotonous similarity" of patriarchal constraints. *Feminist Economics*, *22*(1), 295–321. https://doi.org/10.1080/13545701.2015.1090009

Kabeer, N. (2017). Economic pathways to women's empowerment and active citizenship: What does the evidence from Bangladesh tell us? *The Journal of Development Studies*, *53*(5), 649–663. https://doi.org/10.1080/00220388.2016. 1205730

Kabeer, N. (2020). Women's empowerment and economic development: A feminist critique of storytelling practices in "randomista" economics. *Feminist Economics*, *26*(2), 1–26. https://doi.org/10.1080/13545701.2020.1743338

Kabeer, N., & Huq, L. (2010). The power of relationships: Love and solidarity in a landless women's organization in rural Bangladesh. *IDS Bulletin*, *41*(2), 79–87. https://onlinelibrary.wiley.com/doi/pdf/10.1111/j.1759-5436.2010.00126.x?casa_ token=tle5LJHjcOUAAAAA:idJia1c8KJxoAeHxfe88jsjt5PbgYmTzpaUJQyspi XOIeX7uic6xDkji2RFLjwksjNMdOvjGTsoNgWtB

Kabeer, N., Mahmud, S., & Tasneem, S. (2018). The contested relationship between paid work and women's empowerment: Empirical analysis from Bangladesh. *The European Journal of Development Research*, *30*(2), 235–251. https://link. springer.com/content/pdf/10.1057/s41287-017-0119-y.pdf

Lillis, T. M. (2001). *Student writing: Access, regulation, desire*. Routledge.

McEwan, C. (2001). Postcolonialism, feminism and development: Intersections and dilemmas. *Progress in Development Studies*, *1*(2), 93–111. https://journals. sagepub.com/doi/pdf/10.1177/146499340100100201?casa_token=0kQRdQzGu K4AAAAA:UURZFREfGyLG3gxXbhXsq3uy0baNxgqjjzYY_8n2q_5Yqq3jr0E XPEyJyQSJH4aQIiIC5ZmhpnqdxtU

Shikdar, N. B. (2003). Women Garment Workers in Dhaka: Responses From Workers, Employers and Organisers to Local and Global Pressures. The University of Manchester (United Kingdom).

Siddiqi, D. M., & Ashraf, H. M. (2017). Bangladesh: Class, precarity and the politics of care. In *Women, work and care in the Asia-Pacific* (pp. 118–132). Routledge.

Vygotsky, L. S. (1978). *Mind in society. The development of higher psychological processes*. Harvard University Press.

3 The Continued Silencing of Gayatri Spivak's Subaltern

A Critique of the Elite Nexus of NGOs, Academia, and Corporations

Rashedur Chowdhury and Farooq Ahmad

Introduction

We focus on elite non-governmental organizations (NGOs) and the role they play in dominating the subaltern in developing countries. By *subaltern* we mean marginalized people who not only come from lower social classes but also possess vulnerable social identities, racial profiles, and positions in various forms in different contexts (cf. Chowdhury, 2021a; Gramsci, 1971; Spivak, 1988). Thus, they lack human agency to influence institutional settings and are unable to improve their daily lives on their own terms (Chowdhury, 2021b; Spivak, 1988). We define elite NGOs as powerful actors that have legitimacy and resources to influence institutional decision-making (Chowdhury, 2017a). Often, they are supported by foreign aid agencies and multinational corporations (MNCs) or their foundations so that these NGOs exert power and influence on behalf of their powerful counterparts in developing countries (Chowdhury et al., 2018). By considering Spivak's work (e.g., Spivak, 1988, 1994, 2003) we show how current Western-centric neocolonial concepts utilized by elite NGOs are worsening the pre-existing socio-economic inequalities of the subaltern in developing countries rather than improving their situations. We argue that elite NGOs in developing countries have moved away from their original objectives of stimulating social change and gender equality. Instead, they have begun to operate with renewed agendas to achieve power, intervene in governmental decision-making, and engage in corruption, thus creating a powerful nexus of NGO, academia, and corporates to dominate the subaltern.

More specifically, we posit that elite NGOs import neocolonial capitalistic policies into developing countries which not only perpetuates social problems but further pushes the subaltern out of the public sphere. Elite NGOs thus deviate from their primary work of empowering the subaltern, particularly poor women in developing countries. In doing so, elite NGOs gain more political power and try to replace the responsibility of central

DOI: 10.4324/9781003197270-4

governments, thereby creating a "state within a state" which is able to influence and manipulate the elected governments and academia to serve neoliberal agendas. Additionally, these NGOs engage in power politics in ways that serve the individual interests of their owners or executives, while they are simultaneously portrayed by a section of uncritical and biased academics and researchers as the "superheroes" of social change. Such views indicate a dangerous Western-centric knowledge bias which perpetuates the popular but misleading idea that NGOs are exclusively altruistic and virtuous organizations. To counter this dysfunctional worldview, we argue that decolonization in every aspect of life and organization must happen in various ways in a continuous manner toward the intended outcome. For example, it is particularly important for elite NGOs, academia, and corporations to stop promoting self-fulfilling neocolonial ideologies, policies, and practices. By doing so, they can focus their energy, time, and resources to decolonize their own mindsets, attitudes, postures, measures, and initiatives toward the subaltern within and outside their organizations so that, collectively, we confine subalternity to history and ensure that all citizens on this earth enjoy the dignity they deserve in all aspects of their lives.

The Origin of Subaltern and Their Miseries

Gayatri Spivak is a literary theorist, radical thinker, and critic of international civil society organizations and NGOs; she is also one of the pioneers of subaltern studies. The concept of subaltern has its origins in Gramsci's (1971) writing on agrarian peasant workers with weak socio-political consciousness, which has been radically transformed by the Subaltern Studies group. This group initially examined the nature of the subaltern to rural Indian resistance to British colonial rules which was then applied in other fields and contexts (e.g., Kapoor, 2004; Beverley, 1994; Chaturvedi, 2012).

Spivak (1988) has substantiated the discussion of the subaltern by emphasizing the gendered nature of the concept. Spivak's philosophy grew out of an investigation into the socially constructed logic of *sati*, the widow sacrifice practiced in colonial India. She examined the British move to abolish the practice as part of the British mission to impose Western "civilized" ways on India (Kapoor, 2004). This contrasts with the dominant discourse in Hindu society which justified the practice by arguing that the widows wanted to die. Spivak explains how each representation legitimates the other: One purports to represent a social mission, that of saving Hindu women from their own (brown) men; the other presents the practice as a privilege, allowing women to commit a "pure" act. But all the while, the widow's own voice is ignored, and her individual opinion is obliterated by both the patriarchy and imperialism. Spivak also suggests that even when the female subaltern speaks, she cannot be heard. Spivak describes subalterns as

> The margins (one can just as well say the silent, silenced center) of the circuit marked out by this epistemic violence, men and women among the illiterate peasantry, the tribals, the lowest strata of the urban subproletariat.
>
> (Spivak, 1988, p. 78)

Although this narration is all-too-often reduced to the idea of the rural and illiterate women and men of the Global South, Spivak urges her readers not to confine the subaltern to a certain demographic. To her, the meaning is inherently much deeper than this. Spivak thinks about the subaltern in terms of position; the spaces they inhabit wherein they are cut off from social mobility. She explains:

> Subalternity is not a pathetic thing about subaltern folk. It is a description of a political or social position. The subaltern speaks for themselves. So what is the difference between them and any other human beings? . . . [T]he problem is not located in their being deprived of interior life but in having the access to the public sphere so that their resistance can be recognized as such.
>
> (Conversations with Spivak in Chakravorty et al., 2006, pp. 72–73)

The subaltern is not recognizable within the public sphere. Spivak (1988, p. 102) clarifies her use of the word silence to describe this process to which the subaltern is subjected:

> Between patriarchy and imperialism, subject-constitution and object-formation, the figure of the woman disappears, not into a pristine nothingness, but into a violent shuttling which is the displaced figuration of the "third-world woman" caught between tradition and modernization.

The values of Eurocentric discourse exclude the subaltern so that they experience "a violent aporia between subject and object status" (Spivak, 1988, p. 102). It is imperative to understand conceptual dynamics between the subaltern and the so-called public sphere by considering the elite NGOs. Spivak is highly critical and skeptical of the potential of neoliberal elite NGOs to have a positive impact on the subaltern. In Spivak's (2003, p. 38) classic book *Death of a Discipline*, she uses the term "highly gendered and self-styled international civil society" to show divisions between NGOs and the communities which they purport to serve, as well as the ways in which elite NGOs sustain the status quo. She argues that NGO projects do not include the subaltern for whom NGOs implement policies. Rather, the subaltern population is often excluded for reasons such as the inability to write or speak in Eurocentric modes of communication, or a general unwelcomeness, and lack of historic presence within the public sphere. Due to the lack of Eurocentric, liberal, and enlightened knowledge, the subaltern is denied the opportunity for communication or potential to be understood by those who run and manage NGOs. Not so surprisingly, there is always a rift and tension in the relationship between the subaltern and elites, which may be where we also begin to encounter the potential to leave behind violence and embrace practices of ethical social change to the current NGO model (Spivak, 1994, 2009).

Spivak (2003) pushes us to reimagine communication and understanding between the subaltern and the public sphere. She asks us to think beyond the ideas of the neocolonial capitalism of the West, since it hinders the subaltern from direct involvement in institutional decision-making. In contrast, she advocates that we adopt a non-Eurocentric perspective and champion a noncolonial mindset whereby the concept of subalternity as "normal" can be rejected by the subaltern (see also Chowdhury, 2021a, 2021b). This also means dismantling the status quo of elite NGOs so that long-standing patterns of inequality and injustice are addressed effectively. Indeed, the whole notion of charitable giving needs to be challenged as it perpetuates the hierarchical relationship between elite NGOs and the subaltern they serve. What is needed is a model which situates the subaltern at the center of the aid projects and gives them an authentic platform from which they are able to express *their* views, *their* needs, and speak out about the changes *they* want to see (Griffiths, 2018).

Spivak is also critical about NGOs' interventions in developing countries in the name of "democracy," which Spivak (2003, p. 38) considers a "name for the political restricting entailed by the transformation of . . . state capitalisms and their colonies to tributary economies of rationalized global financialization." She believes that NGOs often promote human rights in the name of democracy and try to impose neoliberal agendas and further the hegemonic and colonial order of Western-centric domination in developing countries. This is sustained as networks of elite NGOs can attract support from multinational corporations (MNCs) and Western governments collaborating transnationally to improve the livelihood of the world's citizens. The dominating nature of "network" encourages Western-style democratization in the Global South. But at the same time its inherent motives and final outcomes have negative consequences for the subaltern population in the Global South who lose control of their lives and voice as Western-centric elite networks interfere in the democratic processes in developing countries.

A Discursive Role of Elite NGOs in Silencing the Subaltern

Elite NGOs sustain themselves by creating a discourse which is informed and shaped by the Westernized organizational processes and practices where the subaltern is portrayed as recipients of aid and pity. By interpreting Foucault, Weedon (1987, p. 108) refers to discourse as ways of constituting knowledge, together with the social practices, forms of subjectivity and power relations which inhere in such knowledges and relations between them. Discourses are more than ways of thinking and producing meaning. They constitute the "nature" of the body, unconscious and conscious mind and emotional life of the subjects they seek to govern.

An NGO-led discourse is created and maintained through power and knowledge where elite NGOs dominate their poor clients by allowing their resourceful owners or board members and employees to make decisions. Such use of power – which is labeled as professionalization or key administrative work – eventually helps elite NGOs to impose their neocolonial ideas to exploit poor clients. The need for NGOs appears to have grown out of the discourses of poverty and social change where the subaltern needs to be empowered. Therefore, elite NGOs avoid developing a reciprocal relationship with the subaltern; rather these NGOs alter and (re)shape discourses by adopting the hegemonic nature of organizational norms and values (Chowdhury & Willmott, 2018). In this way, they sustain the status quo to dominate a subaltern population in a given context.

Yapa (2002) demonstrates the role of discourse in sustaining the status quo. Yapa (2002) discusses how conventional wisdom informs us that poverty represents a lack of development and thus, it follows that economic development is seen as the answer to the problem. Hence Yapa (2002, p. 33) highlights: "poverty is a form of scarcity induced by the very process of development" and that "the materiality of the poverty problem does not exist independent of discourses we have constructed to understand it," concluding that "social science could not simply mirror a pre-given world, because the world is constructed by what science describes." If NGOs continue to construct a discourse on helping the subaltern that is beset by underdevelopment, poverty, starvation, and lack of basic services, this discourse will then continue to sustain the need for the apparatus of elite NGOs. This discourse also shapes the power-knowledge regime of these NGOs and, by implication shapes how organizations execute relationships between NGOs and poor clients and, more importantly, foreign donors and corporate investors.

The key point is that elite NGOs sustain themselves on a discourse that they create and build through their organizational culture and practices which ultimately establishes a self-serving mechanism to please their foreign donors and fulfill corporate agendas. The power-knowledge that shapes NGO-led discourse at both national and international levels is dependent on maintaining the poor as a powerless, vulnerable, and voiceless population of society. Hence, their existence relies on the continuation of poverty and inequalities that they want (need) to eradicate which, instead of promoting nonhierarchical learning and community connection, promotes neocolonial agendas to ignore and exclude the subaltern voice in institutional decision-making.

A Nexus of Elite NGOs, Academia, and Corporations in Silencing the Subaltern

Elite NGOs are able to develop a discourse that helps them to attract support from a section of academia and corporations alike to sustain their neoliberal work to silence the subaltern. Below we discuss four ways in which NGOs make use of their networks, connections, and collaboration with selected academics and corporations that often manipulate a system which is supposed to protect the rights and voice of the subaltern.

The Corporatization of NGOs

The recent phenomenon of NGOs becoming corporate entities by implementing business strategies such as the provision of microcredit is the byproduct of the neoliberal capitalist-centric approach, which Spivak (2003, p. 38) terms "economies of rationalized global financialization." *Microcredit* is an element within *microfinance* that provides credit services to poor clients (Al-Amin & Mathbotr, 2019; Mannan, 2009). This discourse focuses on concerns relating to the corporatization of NGOs insofar as it leads to neoliberal microcredit practices in developing countries, since these practices are known to negatively affect the poor (Chowdhury & Willmott, 2018). The prevalence of microcredit schemes in developing countries is particularly worrying, since elite NGOs may vigorously promote a philanthropic front while covertly engaging in profitable business activities (e.g., Chowdhury & Willmott, 2018). In the context of Bangladesh, for instance, elite NGOs receive substantial foreign funding to mobilize microcredit services, resulting in their operation as quasi-corporate entities (Karim, 2011) while the poor become ever more vulnerable to debt and unemployment (Chowdhury & Willmott, 2018).

Proponents of the microcredit discourse (e.g., Mair et al., 2012; Yunus & Jolis, 1998) claim that the process of NGO corporatization enables the poor to free themselves from the shackles of poverty. However, critics (e.g., Chowdhury & Willmott, 2018; Karim, 2008) argue that as soon as micro-credit becomes a form of legitimate, institutionalized business practice for elite NGOs, the process of corporatization opens the door to other profit-able business activities (e.g., Fernando, 2005; Karim, 2008, 2011; Mannan, 2009; Muhammad, 2009, 2015a; Chowdhury, 2017a) and professionaliza-tion. Within these constructs, these NGOs establish an extreme command and control system of managerial hierarchies, skewed accountability, deadlines, and meeting expectations which Spivak (2003, p. 38) criticizes as "impatient philanthropy." In their study, Chowdhury and Willmott (2018) interview Professor Anu Muhammad, an academic activist who demonstrates how the corporatization of NGOs has led to the unregulated expansion of the market via the widespread take-up of microcredit by the poor and marginalized and explains how the resultant cycles of debt drag the subaltern population further down into grinding poverty. Ahmed (2007) notes that 1,189 out of 2,501 respondents were unable to make the repay-ments for their micro-loans on time and that most of the clients resorted to re-borrowing the money at significantly higher interest rates from other lenders, while others were forced to sell their assets to repay their loans (see Chowdhury & Willmott, 2018 for more details).

The negative impact of microcredit was also evident in other parts of the world. For example, in Andhra Pradesh, India, more than 70 people commit-ted suicide between 1 March and 19 November 2010 due to unrealistic loan repayment schemes (Lee & David, 2010). These schemes were intensely encouraged because NGOs (such as SKS, founded in India in 1998, that was floated on the Bombay Stock Exchange in 2010) along with other micro-credit institutions such as L&T Finance, Spandana Sphoorty Financial, and Share Microfin assisted (encouraged) farmers to take on excessive micro-credit. These loans imposed an unbearable burden of repayment on these farmers, which pushed them toward shame, agony, and suicide. This situa-tion reached such a catastrophic level that the regional government in India imposed restrictions on microlender agents' activities by requiring them to secure the local authorities' approval before issuing any new loan.

Unethical Practices of NGOs

Ethnographic studies by Karim (2011) suggest that elite NGOs report a high recovery rate of repayment loans. However, to achieve these figures, it appears that NGOs engage in unethical practices that directly contradict the basic tenets of the NGO as a moral entity. By extension, the small loans offered to the poor for income-generation projects are unethical since such loans are not the magic bullet of poverty alleviation that lenders claim them to be (Chowdhury & Willmott, 2018). Professor Muhammad Younis, who won a joint Nobel Peace Prize for his work on microcredit with the Grameen Bank, describes a unique set of social objectives said to be attainable via microcredit loans. These include the empowerment of women, the promotion of entrepreneurship and self-employment, elimination of human rights abuses, and, most importantly, the building of social capital (Karim, 2011). In theory, this model presents a fascinating win-win method of eliminating poverty and elevating the standard of living for the poor in practice; however, it fails to consider the social and economic realities of the local communities. Portraying a loan as credit is in fact manifesting a lie in the context of developing countries. Such a loan would be better termed a debt trap as it influences the poor to borrow multiple loans to repay the original loan (Karim, 2008).

This situation worsens for women where patriarchal values are dominant. A woman's lack of ability to pay back a loan may bring dishonor to her immediate and extended family as NGO officers often use shame as a tool to force women to repay their loans. For example, a female borrower may be brought to a police station by an NGO officer which can be shameful for her family. In rural Bangladesh, elite NGOs have made use of such tactics which dishonor families and thus create an "economy of shame" (Karim, 2008). Therefore, when NGOs such as Grameen Bank, for instance, claim loan-repayment recovery rates of around 97–98 per cent, it is not difficult to understand how powerful cultural manipulation tactics such as social shaming impose pressure on its poor clients (Karim, 2011). Such tactics are difficult to apply in a developed country (e.g., Grameen's failure to use such tactics; Scotland to collect debts from its clients; Martin, 2018) where a person may file for bankruptcy and NGOs do not have the power to persuade the police to threaten clients for repayments. The BBC (2013) reported that the pressure system in developing countries for repayment is so intense that recipients of microcredits in Bangladesh have been forced to sell their organs to repay loans; there have also been numerous reports of Bangladeshi microcredit agencies acting violently toward poor borrowers (Karim, 2008, 2011; Chowdhury & Willmott, 2018).

Microcredit schemes can therefore be seen as a way to destroy social cohesion as well as undermine traditional inter- and intra-community support systems that the poor often depend on. Arguments for microcredit as a vehicle for poverty alleviation (e.g., Mair et al., 2012; Yunus & Jolis, 1998) are cast in a new and unflattering light. As the veil of benevolence is lifted, such arguments are shown to be deeply problematic, if not altogether empty (Chowdhury & Willmott, 2018). They are seen to form part of a wider, hegemonic discourse (Spivak, 2003) that is advanced through processes of cultural and political manipulation and perpetuated by neoliberal academic knowledge re-production. Other studies have suggested that powerful NGOs have forced borrowers to sell their cyclone relief materials and to use government housing compensation packages to repay their microcredit loans (Chowdhury & Willmott, 2018). The tactics NGOs use to recover loans are clearly contrary to their stated philanthropic philosophies, and they often avoid direct accountability by sub-contracting this role out to small NGOs or local elites and state police who use violence, harassment, and social shaming to extort repayments.

Elite NGOs as a Vehicle to Sustain Corruption and Corporate Power

Neoliberal conceptions that elite NGOs follow often lead to corruption via corporatization and NGO involvement in national power politics, tax avoidance, or international bidding for aid contracts. Although engagement in power politics is certainly not a mandate of elite NGOs, they have become interested in this as it helps to expand their influence in governmental decision-making. For example, in the 1990s, the World Bank legitimized NGO provision of microcredit services in developing countries, and the abundance of foreign funding and government support has resulted in NGO microcredit programs capturing the bigger market, and hence becoming more powerful in local politics. Gaining a share in political decision-making can lead to further weakening of the democratic role of the state and, with it, greater opportunity to manipulate and exert political pressure on the elected government.

Chowdhury and Willmott (2018) investigated how corporatization of NGOs has led to corruption and cite the case of the controversial 2010 Bangladeshi microcredit scandal, where the government found it politically expedient to criticize Professor Yunus but in practice turned a blind eye to the questionable operation and governance of microcredit programs and other NGO activities due to his high-profile position. This kind of selective positioning response severely weakens the likelihood that elite NGOs will be mandated to set up standard corporate governance practices that are required of all other business entities to ensure transparency and accountability.

In addition, elite NGOs often take the opportunity to avoid tax by claiming charitable activities when they are, in fact, running corporate activities. For example, BRAC, the world's largest NGO runs banks, universities, hotels, restaurants, and other business ventures under the guise of charitable status. Henceforth, the apex court in Bangladesh has ruled that BRAC must pay Taka 404.21 crore (approximately US$47,480,770) in income taxes accumulated between 1993 and 2012 (Shaon, 2016). A reasonable question this raises is why and how a court would make such a judgment against an NGO if it (the NGO) was running their activities under charitable status. Obviously, BRAC went beyond its usual NGO activities which influenced a court to deliver such a verdict.

When elite NGOs become powerful, they not only become heavily involved in corporate activities but also may work as agents of MNCs which severely affect the lives of the subaltern (Haque, 2002). For example, in the aftermath of the Rana Plaza collapse, elite NGOs worked in collaboration with multinational clothing companies and helped to develop institutions such as the Accord (led mostly by European MNCs in addition to a few Western NGOs, with the involvement of a few Western and six Bangladeshi trade unions) and Alliance (a similar institution to the Accord, except that its members are mainly US retailers and involve elite NGOs such as BRAC) in Bangladesh. Some of these NGOs also had a significant role to diagnose the nature of injuries and compensate victims who were affected by the Rana Plaza collapse (Chowdhury, 2017a). These victims were supposed to be served by the state and legal mechanisms so that they could be duly compensated. Instead, elite NGOs took on a consultancy role on behalf of Western multinational clothing firms and the Bangladesh government turned a blind eye to this process of allowing such consultancy work rather than adequately mobilizing state-run organizations to help the victims (Chowdhury, 2017a). More worryingly, some academics (e.g., Reinecke & Donaghey, 2015, 2021a, 2021b) were in praise of MNCs because they were signatories of Accord which brought a few Bangladeshi trade unions in on such an agreement. While trade unions may represent a good number of marginalized workers in some parts of Europe, some of the Bangladeshi trade unions affiliated to the Accord for instance have political affiliations, which makes it hard to see how they can be truly representative of the subaltern worker population (Nuruzzaman, 2006; Rahman & Langford, 2014; Shifa et al., 2015; Taher, 1999). For example, the six trade unions listed in the Accord may be affiliated with either the ruling party or the main opposition party. Often NGOs and trade unions in Bangladesh are formed to encourage popularity in order to protect political party and business interests, which are intertwined (Rahman & Langford, 2014; Shifa et al., 2015; Sumon, 2016). Further, it is not clear who made the decision and what criteria were used to select these six trade unions (for instance, were they proposed by MNCs, NGOs, or Western trade unions?). If elite NGOs or Western trade unions were consulted to select local trade unions, naturally a question of these actors' legitimacy arises because these actors do not have a mandate from the Bangladeshi workers to dictate their lives.

Unfortunately, some academics did not understand that Accord and Alliance were developed so that public focus deviates from a compensation process for poor workers (Chowdhury, 2017a; Muhammad, 2015b). If legal procedures were maintained and the state took adequate legal actions against MNCs, these MNCs had to pay a hefty compensation. Rather than doing that, later, some of the MNCs that were signatories of Accord and Alliance started claiming that they have created a cooperative environment where these marginalized workers had more voice and rights (e.g., Reinecke & Donaghey, 2021a). Numerous academic works and reports (e.g., Alamgir et al., 2021; Human Rights Watch, 2021; Grant & Carroll, 2020), however, show that Bangladeshi workers are still in a dire state and lack basic human rights in the workplace. Instead, a greenwashing mechanism (Chowdhury, 2019) is in place to claim that marginalized workers are capable of talking with powerful actors and have the ability to influence positive changes through dialogs with MNCs or elite NGOs. However, this is a situation which does not exist at all particularly given that fast fashion is still a dominant driving force in the clothing industry. Moreover, in the current environment, it is impossible for female workers to speak out in any form as they are marginalized, brutalized, and silenced by the powerful nexus of MNCs, elite NGOs, and the complicit behavior of the Bangladesh government and some Western academics who are strong supporters of neo-colonial conceptions that oppress the workers in the name of unionization. While a true unionization is welcome, a romantic tale of inventing the existence of unions in developing countries is unethical and dangerous because it silences these female workers in extreme ways.

Academic Imperialism

Academics and researchers who are trained in Western institutions often have little or no knowledge of cultural dynamics and local realities (Spivak, 1994; Spivak & Harasym, 1990). Spivak (1994) challenges researchers who believe without question that they are drawing accurate conclusions from the data they have chosen to collect and analyze to think again, since most of them are operating from biased perspectives of Western-centric academic culture and traditions. Spivak substantiates this argument (see Spivak & Harasym, 1990) by maintaining that researchers from Western universities visit developing countries for fieldwork and data collection to serve personal and institutional interests (a notion supported by empirical work, e.g., Crewe & Harrison, 1998; Khan, 2001). She refers to this process as imperialistic "information retrieval" (Spivak, 1988, p. 90), wherein the developing countries become a "repository of an ethnographic 'cultural difference'" (Spivak, 1999, p. 388). To her, this ultimately helps Western institutions to take control of the production of knowledge (Spivak, 1994).

By following Spivak (1994, 1999), we further argue that obviously some academics may like to believe that they are adding value to current theories that rely on Western philosophical tradition, yet all the while they may be blatantly ignorant of or gloss over the experiences and concerns of the subaltern population they wish to investigate or make claims on behalf of This is worst when Western philosophy does not fit neatly into pre-existing frameworks of reference that academics want to use for their understanding of the subaltern, and, therefore, they naively misinterpret the subaltern experience in the first place. Thereafter, they report the subaltern experience in academic journals and NGO/corporate reports in a way that helps powerful organizations such as elite NGOs and MNCs to benefit from academic work (in worst cases, from consultancy work which academics undertake with NGOs and corporations). In other words, it is the subaltern experience which is neglected or denied repeatedly and systemically (Kapoor, 2004). This misrepresentation will perpetuate as long as academics fail to immerse themselves into the subaltern experience and continue to make assumptions about the subaltern perspectives through the lens of dominant NGOs and corporations which are then evaluated in terms of how they fit with the Western dualities of theory and practice (Chowdhury, 2020, 2017b). This is a colossal issue given that academics based in Western institutions often have more resources and power to abuse academic language in academic and public outlets than anyone else (Chowdhury, 2021b). Often, these academics even have the freedom to write numerous papers which can violate the dignities of the subaltern repeatedly (Chowdhury, 2021a).

Ultimately, a production of Western-centric theory has implications for practice which is never free from bias. This perpetuates as academics often collaborate with elite NGOs or corporations in the name of consultancy or simply to gain data from NGO sites or network with MNCs through NGOs, or vice versa. In this way, they (consciously or unconsciously) help sustain a network of powerful actors and their nexus to reap benefits and maximize profits. We contend that such nexus – that is, where academics are reliant on elite NGOs and MNCs for data collection and interpretation of subaltern experience – is a *vicious process* of silencing the voice of the subaltern.

Conclusion

Currently, elite NGOs practice neocolonial strategies and policies which, instead of bringing social change for the betterment of the subaltern in developing countries, disempower them. However, one must not forget that Western-centric neocolonial concepts do not operate in a vacuum. For example, perversely, they actually rely on the failure of developing country governments to provide basic infrastructures of healthcare, education, employment, and equality for the subaltern. Once NGOs gain a foothold by offering social and educational programs to address these needs, they become more powerful in intervening in government decision-making, which often undermines the functionalities of public institutions. Thus, in developing countries, it is the elite rather than the subaltern who benefit from neocolonial agendas, and the voices of the subaltern remain unacknowledged and unheard even when they speak out.

We argue that there is indeed a need for NGOs to act urgently with academics and corporations to decolonize their approaches with the consent of the subaltern. The consent, however, should not be gained through violence, threats, or hegemonic behavior. It essentially means that, for the NGOs to align themselves more effectively with the subaltern, the nexus of NGO, academia, and corporations needs to break free from the current mode of neocolonialization. For this, academics need to be highly critical of neocolonial policies and practices. Some of them also need to *break free from the elite corporate and NGO nexus* from which they often benefit by accessing NGO or corporate sites and portray the organizations they research in a positive light. If accountability and transparency among academics, NGOs, and corporations is established, then the subaltern can have a more dignified daily life, enjoy access to equal opportunities, and participate in democratic processes and decision-making. It is only then that we may have a real opportunity to fully eliminate the very idea of subalternity. Otherwise, the endurance of subaltern pain and suffering will continue, and none of us will be able to make peace with the guilt we hold about the draconian and cruel moral violations we often impose on the most vulnerable populations of the Global South.

References

Ahmed, Q. (2007). *Some findings on microcredit at micro level: Socio-economic and indebtedness-related impact of microcredit in Bangladesh*. University Press Limited.

Alamgir, F., Alamgir, F., & Irina Alamgir, F. (2021). Live or be left to die? Deregulated bodies and the global production network: Expendable workers of the Bangladeshi apparel industry in the time of Covid. *Organization*. doi:10.1177/13505084211028528

Al-Amin, M., & Mathbor, G. M. (2019). Agency, empowerment and intra-household gender relations in Bangladesh: Does market-oriented microcredit contribute? *Asian Journal of Women's Studies, 25*, 258–284.

BBC. (2013, October 28). The Bangladesh poor selling organs to pay. *BBC Asia*. http:// www.bbc.com/news/world-asia-24128096.

Beverley, J. (1994). Writing in reverse: On the project of the Latin American subaltern studies group. *Dispositio, 19*, 271–288.

Chakravorty, S., Milevska, S., & Barlow, T. E. (2006). *Conversations with Gayatri Chakaravorty [ie Chakravorty] spivak*. Seagull.

Chaturvedi, V. (Ed.). (2012). *Mapping subaltern studies and the postcolonial*. Verso Books

Chowdhury, R. (2017a). The Rana Plaza disaster and the complicit behavior of elite NGOs. *Organization, 24*(6), 938–949.

Chowdhury, R. (2017b). Rana Plaza fieldwork and academic anxiety: Some reflections. *Journal of Management Studies, 54*, 1111–1117.

Chowdhury, R. (2019). (In)sensitive violence, development, and the smell of the soil: Strategic decision-making of what? *Human Relations, 74*(1), 131–152.

Chowdhury, R. (2020). The mobilization of noncooperative spaces: Reflections from Rohingya refugee camps. *Journal of Management Studies*. doi:10.1111/joms.12612

Chowdhury, R. (2021a). Self-representation of marginalized groups: A new way of thinking through W. E. B. Du Bois. *Business Ethics Quarterly, 31*(4), 524–548.

Chowdhury, R. (2021b). From black pain to Rhodes must fall: A rejectionist perspective. *Journal of Business Ethics, 170*, 287–311.

Chowdhury, R., Kourula, A., & Siltaoja, M. (2018). Power of paradox: Grassroots organizations' legitimacy strategies over time. *Business and Society, 60*(2), 420–453.

Chowdhury, R., & Willmott, H. (2018). Microcredit, the corporatization of NGOs and academic activism: The example of Professor Anu Muhammad. *Organization, 26*(1), 122–140.

Crewe, E., & Harrison, E. (1998). *Whose development? An ethnography of aid*. Zed Books.

Fernando, J. L. (Ed.). (2005). *Perils and prospects of micro-credit: Neoliberalism and cultural politics of empowerment*. Routledge.

Gramsci, A. (1971). *Selections from the prison notebooks*. Lawrence and Wishart.

Grant, H., & Carroll, J. (2020, August 7). Covid to 'brutal crackdown 'on garment workers' rights. *The Guardian*. www.theguardian.com/global-development/2020/aug/07/covid-led-to-brutal-crackdown-on-garment-workers-rights-says-report

Griffiths, M. (2018). For speaking against silence: Spivak's subaltern ethics in the field. *Transactions of the Institute of British Geographers, 43*, 299–311.

Haque, M. S. (2002). The changing balance of power between the government and NGOs in Bangladesh. *International Political Science Review, 23*, 411–435.

Human Rights Watch. (2021). *Bangladesh: Events of 2020*. www.hrw.org/world-report/2021/country-chapters/bangladesh

Kapoor, I. (2004). Hyper-self-reflexive development? Spivak on representing the third world 'other'. *Third World Quarterly, 25*, 627–647.

Karim, L. (2008). Demystifying micro-credit: The Grameen Bank, NGOs, and neoliberalism in Bangladesh. *Cultural Dynamics, 20*, 5–29.

Karim, L. (2011). *Microfinance and its discontents: Women in debt in Bangladesh*. University of Minnesota Press.

Khan, S. (2001). Performing the native informant: Doing ethnography from the margins. *Canadian Journal of Women and the Law, 13*(2), 266–284.

Lee, Y., & David, R. (2010, December 28). Suicides in India revealing how men made a mess of microcredit. *Bloomberg.* www.bloomberg.com/news/articles/2010-12-28/suicides-amongborrowers-in-india-show-how-men-made-a-mess-of-microcredit

Mair, J., Marti, I., & Ventresca, M. J. (2012). Building inclusive markets in rural Bangladesh: How intermediaries work in institutional voids. *Academy of Management Journal, 55*, 819–850.

Mannan, M. (2009). BRAC: Anatomy of a "poverty enterprise". *Nonprofit Management and Leadership, 20*, 219–233.

Martin, G. (2018, December 20). Scottish micro-lending charity collapses. *TFN.* https://tfn.scot/news/scottish-micro-lending-charity-collapses

Muhammad, A. (2009). Grameen and microcredit: A tale of corporate success. *Economic and Political Weekly, 44*(35), 35–42.

Muhammad, A. (2015a, March 1). Bangladesh – a model of neoliberalism. *Monthly Review.* https://monthlyreview.org/2015/03/01/bangladesh-a-model-of-neoliberalism/

Muhammad, A. (2015b). Workers' lives, Walmart's pocket: Garments' global chain, from Savar to New York. *Economic & Political Weekly, 25*, 143–150.

Nuruzzaman, M. (2006). Labor resistance to pro-market economic reforms in Bangladesh. *Journal of Asian and African Studies, 41*(4), 341–357.

Rahman, Z., & Langford, T. (2014). International solidarity or renewed trade union imperialism? The AFL-CIO and garment workers in Bangladesh. *The Journal of Labor and Society, 17*(2), 169–186.

Reinecke, J., & Donaghey, J. (2015). After rana plaza: Building coalitional power for labour rights between unions and (consumption-based) social movement organisations. *Organization, 22*(5), 720–740.

Reinecke, J., & Donaghey, J. (2021a). Transnational representation in global labour governance and the politics of input legitimacy. *Business Ethics Quarterly.* doi:10.1017/beq.2021.27

Reinecke, J., & Donaghey, J. (2021b). Political CSR at the coalface – the roles and contradictions of multinational corporations in developing workplace dialogue. *Journal of Management Studies, 58*, 457–486.

Shaon, A. I. (2016, August 4). Brac to pay Tk404 crore in taxes. *Dhaka Tribune.* www.dhakatribune.com/bangladesh/2016/08/04/brac-pay-tk404-crore-taxes

Shifa, N., Gulrukh, S., & Sumon, M. (2015, May 1). Is the new model of trade unions the answer? *The Daily Star.* www.thedailystar.net/op-ed/politics/the-new-model-trade-unions-the-answer-79997

Spivak, G. C. (1988). Can the subaltern speak? In C. Nelson & L. Grossberg (Eds.), *Marxism and the interpretation of culture* (pp. 271–313). University of Illinois Press.

Spivak, G. C. (1994). Responsibility. *Boundary 2, 21*(3), 19–64.

Spivak, G. C. (1999). *A critique of postcolonial reason: Toward a critique of the vanishing present.* Harvard University Press.

Spivak, G. C. (2003). *Death of a discipline.* Columbia University Press.

Spivak, G. C. (2009). They the people. *Radical Philosophy, 157*, 31–36.

Spivak, G. C., & Harasym, S. (Eds.). (1990). *The post-colonial critic: Interviews, strategies, dialogues*. Routledge.

Sumon, M. H. (2016, April 24). The accord and alliance: Beyond state governance? *The Daily Star*. www.thedailystar.net/op-ed/beyond-state-governance-1213585

Taher, M. A. (1999). Politicization of trade unions: Issues and challenges in Bangladesh perspective. *Indian Journal of Industrial Relations, 34*(4), 403–420.

Weedon, C. (1987). *Feminist practice and poststructuralist theory*. Wiley-Blackwell.

Yapa, L. (2002). How the discipline of geography exacerbates poverty in the third world. *Futures, 34*, 33–46.

Yunus, M., & Jolis, A. (1998). *Banker to the poor*. Aurum Press.

Part II
Exposing Neocolonialism in the Post-colonies

An Urge for Ethics of Care

4 Colonialism Otherwise

Reading Uzma Falak's Kashmir

Ayesha Masood and Sadhvi Dar

Introduction

Postcolonial and feminist critiques on Management and Organization Studies (MOS) have highlighted how universalizing, and ahistorical rationales in MOS knowledge production dehistoricize and de-politicize organizational phenomena by either subsuming postcolonial MOS within Western logics (Mir, 2003; Cooke, 2003) or, in more sinister ways, entirely erasing the post-colony as a differentiated geopolitical arrangement thus silencing knowledge that provides counter-hegemonic narratives (Alcadipani et al., 2012; Masood & Nisar, 2020). At the same time, there is limited engagement from within MOS about the ongoing, everyday forms of postcolonialism, where coloniality is grafted onto bodies and organizing practices through familial and institutional structures. More importantly, there is a limited understanding of how post-colony mediates and instrumentalizes coloniality through hegemonic organizational processes, using the language of managing, markets, and business interests.

To this end, this chapter develops a decolonial feminist praxis to engage with how the post-colony exerts its colonial interests through familial structures and embodied knowledge. Here, we use dual autoethnographic accounts to illustrate how postcolonial state formation is subject to continuous violence over its constituents. Through this, we highlight how our gendered subjectivities are innately connected to hegemonic discourses and registers so we may recover alternate routes to *azaadi* – a radical praxis of decolonizing otherwise. Our methodology extends the work of the Kashmiri feminist anti-colonial poet, Uzma Falak, whose poetry uses the politics of memorialization and bearing witness to give form and visibility to the struggle of subjugated peoples of Kashmir and Kashmiri women's activism.

DOI: 10.4324/9781003197270-6

Knowing Bodies and the Postcolonial Imagination

Postcolonial theory comprises interdisciplinary and multidisciplinary approaches to the study of colonial history and its continued material, social, and cultural manifestations beyond independence (Prasad, 2012). This school of thought emerged after a period of rapid decolonization that was followed by the establishment of neocolonial power relations both among the postcolonial states and their former colonizers, as well as, within former colonial states among white and non-white communities (Yousfi, 2021). In this political context, critical scholars developed a rigorous critique of "western" ontology and epistemology, building a movement with multiple geographic fronts but with shared demands for political recognition (Said, 1978; Bhabha, 2015; Mignolo, 2011). The establishment of postcolonial studies as an academic field of critical thought and theory-building was therefore both the outcome of dedicated activism and an act of community-building that established a space for radical politics in the conservative institutional space of academia (Mignolo, 2007, 2011).

Within MOS, postcolonial critique has highlighted the colonial underpinning of diverse management practices and fields such as corporate social responsibility (Banerjee, 2008; Khan & Lund-Thomsen, 2011), diversity management (Prasad et al., 1997; Jack et al., 2011), development (Cooke, 2010; Srinivas, 2009), knowledge production and transfer (Nkomo, 1992; Mir et al., 2008), and entrepreneurship (Martinez Dy & Jayawarna, 2020). It has also highlighted how hybridity and mimicry produce new forms, practices, and subjectivities in organizations while retaining colonial orders of power and subjugation (Frenkel, 2008, Dar, 2014; Yousfi, 2014). At the same time, scholars in central and south America have provided incisive critiques of North American hegemony over the very conceptual tools and epistemic foundations of MOS knowledge (Ibarra-Colado, 2006; Faria, 2013, Mandiola, 2010).

Despite these important contributions that have deepened our understanding of power relations in the world today, there are still important silences and slippages in research agendas. First, is the fact that postcolonial theory (with very few exceptions) remains focused on the binary encounter between the Global North West (as the colonizers) and the Global South East (as the colonized). As multiple scholars have already noted (Shohat, 1992; Ahmad, 1997; Banerjee, 2000; Osuri & Zia, 2020), this leaves limited space to understand the experiences of local populations that are doubly colonized by neocolonial corporations and the ex-colonized nation-states. Similarly, pinning postcolonial critique to the colonial experience at a specific time and location does not allow us to understand and theorize the ongoing forms of imperialism and colonization, especially those mediated by transgenerational and multi-sited knowledge production (Walsh, 2016;

Bachelard, 1998; Banerjee & Osuri, 2000). As a result, there is limited space to understand, document, and theorize about the experiences of colonialism and conflict that are mediated along other axes, especially inside the postcolonial states.

Second, the perpetuation of colonialism by the post-colonies almost always intersects with and is articulated in the language of management and business development. This is perhaps most apparent in the use of development aid for geopolitical interests asserted by BRICS nations (Gulrajani & Faure, 2019; Thompson, 2019). Colonialism is also more subtly deployed against the racial, classed, and ethnic minorities in the name of opening new markets, creating more transparent financial structures, protecting business interests, or digitalizing economies (Banerjee & Linstead, 2001; Abraham & Rajadhiyaksha, 2015; De Maria, 2008). Supplementing this aim is the insidious mobilization of state administration using identity papers or citizen registries in the name of preventing illegal immigration, documentation of land rights to supposedly facilitate new economies, or banning religious or ethnic practices to create a unitary identity (Banerjee & Linstead, 2001). These are just some examples of the ways post-colonies use imperialist administration within their borders to curtail citizenship, cultural identities, and economic networks of minorities and marginalized communities (Osuri, 2018; Chapparban, 2020).

Finally, some of the existing work on post/decolonial theory examines the colonial experiences at the level of social structures and discourses, which are often produced or subverted through macro level negotiations. Other scholars have sought to look at how colonialism is operationalized in everyday life, especially within families and intimate relations (Ahmed, 2013). We extend this latter thread by investigating how those living with ongoing neocolonialism and its aftermath create new subjectivities. For example, the shifting legal mechanisms inhibiting equal trade and movement, transformative geopolitical power dynamics that entrench opposition to anti-colonial struggles, and new social imaginaries that are increasingly majoritarian and uniformly aligned with right-wing politics are all factors that call for ongoing ontological investigations. This is an important insight, especially given the pervasive nature of social media which individualizes the politics of struggle. We now set out our conceptual framework to address the challenges of theorizing the post-colony.

Colonialism Otherwise: Outline of a Decolonial Feminist Praxis

Colonialism otherwise is specific to the postcolonial state that builds a unitary identity, legal framework, and bureaucratic state apparatus that asserts militaristic nationalism. This configuration is inherently contradictory and complex because it is legitimized by and produced through its historic anti-colonial struggles for self-determination. However, to create a unitary identity (where none may exist) and maintain its (artificially created) geographical borders, postcolonial states reproduce pre-colonial structures of power, while grafting their contemporary forms onto colonial political actions targeting and subjugating specific minorities. As such, *colonialism otherwise* promotes and provokes the subjugation of minorities and minoritized people, enabling and enforcing an unaccountable postcolonial order.

We conceptualize a *colonialism otherwise* because of the current condition of world systems: with the ascent of transnational corporations and boundless financial capitalism, it is no longer possible to attribute or locate the global organization of colonialism within a state (even a developed one). Importantly, the experience of colonialism has inexorably and irrevocably changed the local histories of postcolonial states. To create a unitary identity and/or artificially created state borders, often premised on constructed visions of pre-colonial pasts, post-colonies replicate the governing logics of their previous masters. They have maintained, even strengthened, the constitutional and bureaucratic state apparatuses which are premised on controlling the population and occupying territories, rather than enabling the rights to self-determination through democratic participation (Duschinski & Ghosh, 2017). In this way, the neo-imperialist states like their erstwhile masters continue the vicious oppression of those who struggle against the state, displaying the same coloniality of power as the Europeans, by reproducing their contemporary states of existence through governing life formally through the state and through more subtle forms of state power that appear in familial formations, everyday discourses, and ways of life (Bhan & Duschinski, 2020; Ghosh & Duschinski, 2020; Osuri, 2018).

This situation is perhaps best exemplified by the postcolonial states of India and Pakistan that have been critiqued as patriarchal and militarized formations that reproduce British colonial mechanisms to subjugate minorities as well as to establish the moral premise for denying the self-determination of those subjugated minorities (Kazi, 2014). As such, these states have been more invested in reinforcing militarized aspects of the Westphalian nation-state, rather than strengthening democratic institutions where sovereignty is contested. The interrelatedness of territory, military border control, and gender violence are specific to the "unitary" model for sovereignty, and as such the possibility for an international legal approach to restoring minorities legal rights and protections is mitigated (Kazi, 2014; Ghosh & Duschinski, 2020; Zia, 2019). In a context where identities fracture along lines of decolonized and colonized, accountability for ongoing military violence and systemic religious-racial injustice remain elusive to Kashmiri people (Kazi, 2014; Zia, 2019).

Coming Together and Reading Kashmir

It is important to delineate the process through which we composed the dual autoethnography that engages with Falak's work. As co-authors, we write in relation to what our bodies know and what they do not know. We started a dialogue with each other to share this embodied knowledge in an act of revealing and de-centering institutional discourses that celebrate the postcolonial state as a militarized and triumphant example of independence, freedom, and justice (Anzaldúa, 1987). In this way, we develop the methodology used by Uzma Falak that creates resistance to the idea of linear history and nationhood. As she bears witness to Kashmiri suffering, death, torture, resistance, defiance, and self-love her works of memorialization appear as bricolage – a performative archive that intentionally crisscrosses temporalities, bringing life and death into an uneasy tension with each other. Following Falak (2020b), the narratives we provide later are acts of remembering what is remembered, what is forgotten, and what is possible in terms of imagining Kashmir otherwise. In this way, these accounts show the postcolonial state as operationalized through our bodies rather than an attempt to provide the reader with an objective account of Kashmir.

We want to emphasize that this choice is intentional. As scholars and postcolonial women who have never visited Kashmir, we question the politics that enable us to write about Kashmir. Both of us, in different ways, enjoy the privileged positions of being citizens in our respective states, our understanding of violence in Kashmir has always been mediated by familial narratives and state representations. In some ways, we consented to the violence mediated by the state, making us both perpetrators and victims of *colonialism otherwise*. Thus, speaking *for* Kashmiris would be a continuation of colonialism: it would be a vicious form of appropriating a revolutionary and anti-colonial politics of resistance.

In this chapter, we use Falak's methodology to deal with our fractured solidarity with each other and with Kashmir. Following Falak (2015a), we create a mosaic of memories, visualizations, and sounds to understand how the postcolonial state is operationalized through memory, bodies, emotion, and familial relations. These are our memoryscapes (Kappler, 2017), not formal histories but a combination of oral history and lived memories tinged with emotions. We attempt to challenge the state-sanctioned narratives of Kashmir by reflecting on what our bodies know – the multiple interstates that are made clearer by recollecting diverse histories, embodiments, geographies, and memories about Kashmir. The memoryscapes that follow were remembered and written separately; we come together in the section called Azaadi to account for this act of dialogical memorization.

Heaven on Earth

The earliest memories that I have of Kashmir are acts of memorialization, some of them state sanctions, others more private. One of them is of an assembly held at a private home in memory of Kashmiri martyrs on Kashmir day (held in Pakistan on the 5th of every February). Women from my neighborhood, all with solemn expressions, gathered and listened to speakers: a woman who has recently crossed the line of control to recount her journey, another who read from a book of poetry, another who spoke at length on geopolitical importance of Kashmir and emphasized the shared identity and religion. Such gatherings and events in my history are part of the mythology of Kashmir. Through them, I got to know Kashmir as an idea, a lost land, a lost people, and a never-healing colonial wound. Events like these, and they are still part of everyday Pakistani life, are part of a state-mediated narrative of Kashmir, through which Pakistani people like me come to know of Kashmir.

In many ways, however, this is also how Kashmir becomes unknown. As Falak (2016a) notes, these state-created memories of Kashmir have no bearing on the actual lived experiences or memories of people living in Kashmir Through this, Kashmir is reduced to an "*exotic and as a paradisiacal setting of romance and fantasy*" (Falak, 2016a), and the lived experiences and memories of its people become unknowable and forgotten. I come to understand that the very identity of being Pakistani is intertwined with this mythology of Kashmir. Through the affective memories created by the governing apparatuses of family and state, this mythology is how my knowing and feeling is structured. Kashmir becomes a part of mine, and every Pakistani's, everyday life through these commonplace acts of remembrance. The official state news, watched together as a family and discussed at dinner tables, always contained a section dedicated to news about Indian-held Kashmir, in a way showcasing the misery of people being killed, raped, and oppressed in Kashmir. There were always programs and news broadcasted in Kashmiri language. All through my childhood, there was a constant presence of Kashmir in media, through fictionalized stories, drama, and theatrical productions and songs. Finally, Kashmir Solidarity Day, held on February 5 was always marked with special programming about *Azaadi* movement, haunting songs and heart-wrenching stories of Kashmir. The memories and affect created by and through these accounts undergird my understanding and relationship with Kashmir. Perhaps that is why my feelings toward Kashmir are neither political nor rational. They are affective, mediated through the bricolage of songs, images, and emotions.

Pakistani people weave their identities and affective connections through nationalistic storytelling and memorialization, done through popular literature, art, drama, and poetry. For me, it is important to uncover what is lost, forgotten, and made absent in this affect created by the state. Through these discourses, the land of Kashmir is repositioned and appropriated as a religious symbol of Heaven on Earth (*Fidous bur Zameen*). This religious discourse is then used to highlight that Kashmir is a Muslim-majority region, and therefore its rightful place is with Pakistan. Consequently, Pakistani discourse on Kashmir is replete with religious symbolism: Pakistan's association and solidarity with Kashmir is often articulated through religious terms; Kashmir is considered a symbolic heaven, a pure land; its annexation with Pakistan is considered a right ordained by God; and rendering any aid to Kashmiris and removing infidel Indian army from this pure heavenly land becomes a religious duty. Similar to this religious symbolism is the discourses of Kashmir's strategic and geopolitical importance for the region, especially Pakistan: That Kashmir is Pakistan's jugular vein, an analogy that refers to the strategic and geopolitical importance of the rivers Indus and Jhelum which irrigate most of Pakistan's arable land and dams constructed on them are the major source of hydroelectrical power.

However, despite these discourses and affective connections that Pakistani people feel for Kashmir, ordinary Pakistani can do nothing for Kashmiri people except witness their suffering. As a result, an ordinary Pakistani's relationship with Kashmir is based on feelings of profound disempowerment, helplessness, and guilt: a religious guilt on their inability to purify their holy land, a patriarchal guilt because they cannot avenge or resist the oppression of Kashmiri people, and an emasculated chauvinist guilt because they can only witness the plight of Kashmiri women and cannot rush to their rescue. However, this guilt is like the gilded and broken bodies invoked by Falak (2016a). Our eyes are drawn by the spectacle of the misery of Kashmiri people, and they are held by our own inability to do anything except be a voyeur to their suffering.

To me, the spectacle created by the state discourses around Kashmir is the ultimate betrayal of masculine chauvinistic nationalism of Pakistan's military industry complex. The collective guilt in Pakistani people is created and periodically fueled by military funded and sponsored events, media productions, and programs, to create a populist sentiment against India and to keep Pakistani people in constant fear of invasion. The bond of an artificial solidarity is thus created within Pakistani people. The plight of Kashmiri people, especially ongoing shelling and border skirmishes in Pakistan-held Kashmir are used to justify constantly increasing and unchecked military expenditure, even in times of extreme economic austerity. Most importantly, this leads to military occupation of Pakistan's democratic institutions where Pakistan's internal and foreign policies must always account for military's political ambitions. Any criticism from politicians or from media, or any attempt to make any peaceful overtures to India almost instantaneously lead to charges of sedition and "*baghawat*" (rebellion against the state).

Multiple researchers on military spending suggest that the Pakistan army gains its cultural and social capital by staking its claim over the bodies and land of Kashmir. Through this capital, they are able to retain a large share of Pakistan's budget which is in turn used to fund a huge military-industrial complex (Aziz, 2007). This "milibus" allows military-industrial complex to fund its ever-expanding real estate, banking, agricultural, and food businesses, many of which openly use names like "Askari," Fauji," and "defense" to invoke their connection with the military. Any opposition from farmers, industrialists, or local communities against the forced eviction or land acquisitions is forcefully and violently suppressed (Murphy, 2013; Akhtar, 2006).

However, to me, the most saddening aspect of my relationship with Kashmir is my own deeply felt solidarity with Kashmiri, which I now know to be premised on falsehood of nationalism. Unlike the traditional flavor of colonialism which works on creating the superiority of certain races and regions and alienation of others, this colonialism 2.0 functions by creating artificial bonds of kinship and imaginary solidarity. I feel that my relationship to Kashmir is based on a shared sense of solidarity and struggle against oppression, except any kinship that I feel is false, any solidarity that I feel is almost never for the Kashmiri people themselves. This solidarity and brotherhood masks my complicity in the nationalist project of Pakistani identity. Because of this manufactured affect, the oft-heard Kashmiri slogan "*Hum kya chahte? Azaadi*" in Pakistani ears becomes synonymous with Kashmir's annexation with Pakistan.

Importantly, I understand that my solidarity is created and manufactured through the effective governance, whereby the feeling structures, rules of knowing, and norms of kindship are patterned through and by state and family. On the one hand, this governance determines how everyday Pakistanis feel about Kashmir, and by extension toward their own military and political leaders and Pakistan's relationship with India. On the other hand, ordinary Pakistanis have no way of comprehending or acknowledging that within its own borders Pakistan is equally complicit in oppressing Kashmiris within its own borders and denying them their democratic and political rights. Pakistan's treatment (gilded by the nationalistic agenda) of Pakistan-held Kashmir is only used to claim a moral high ground from India, and thus justify Pakistani's moral claim to Kashmiris and their loyalty.

The final axis of this manufactured affect, created memories, and imagined solidarity is a profound numbness. The solidarity and kinship premised on the impotent chauvinistic guilt does not produce a will to action or even a will to love. It does not lead to any generative or critical discourse. It only leads to a collective feeling of disempowerment, which in the face of conditions faced by the Kashmiri people is nothing but a glorified form of brown guilt. It only allows Pakistanis like me to claim higher moral standards (than India perhaps), absolve us of any responsibility towards Kashmiris within our own borders and stake our claims a little further on Kashmiri land. This, I feel is the last betrayal of affective governance. Whatever I know, think, or feel about Kashmir and its people will always be tinged by the structural and affective structures of produced by state/family complex. In the end, I am left with a question: Is it even possible to imagine a radically different form of solidarity with Kashmir?

Aryan Valley

> *"When someone asks you where you are from,*
> *don't tell them you are a Kashmiri Pandit"*

As an ethnoreligious identity, the Kashmiri Pandit describes a sect of Hindus from Kashmir; all Kashmiri Hindus are said to be upper caste, they are Brahmins or "Pandits." This identity has become increasingly politicized because of the ongoing violence in the region and the minority status that is awarded to Kashmiri Pandits in a Muslim-majority state. Hindu state nationalists have used this minority status to claim that the territory is under threat of capture by Muslim forces, namely Pakistan (Kaul, 2013), and also to use the status symbolically as a sign of Hindu fragility vis-à-vis a muscular Muslim threat.

Territory and identity have become increasingly diffused, re-fused, and used to create anxieties among Kashmiri Pandits, as well as Hindus in the broader sense. I remember as a very young girl, being told by my grandfather that I must never disclose my identity to anyone. Despite our home being in London, he was deeply concerned about what I might say in front of my school friends and how conversations about my ethnicity and religion may lead to violence against me – specifically the threat of being kidnapped by terrorists or other malign forces. Paradoxically, this identity was also a source of great pride and I recall family anecdotes, statements, and conversations about our uniqueness, importance, and significance as Kashmiris to India's identity. As a postcolonial child growing up in the UK, these stories were fundamental to my capacity to resist the virulent and widespread white supremacist racism of the times. This paradox structured an identity on the cusp of collapse because it was full of inconsistencies, re-narration, and forgetting.

Part of our uniqueness was articulated through the culinary practice of making specialty dishes –Kashmiri cuisine has a reputation for its richness, use of specific spices, and indulgent use of lamb (or goat) dishes. Unlike other regions, meat is cooked without the use of onions or garlic that are said to be impure or aphrodisiac – by removing these elements from the preparation of meat, the Brahmin body is supposedly left untainted by the consumption of meat. Yet, inconsistencies about this purity or saintliness were regularly exposed when the family would sit down and remember the gossip and scandals of post-independence. I vividly recall my grandmother telling stories about the politician, Jawaharlal Nehru, who was a Kashmiri Pandit and later India's first Prime Minister. His extramarital affairs, especially with the Viceroy's wife, were shared as a source of entertainment but also to assert that the Kashmiris are innately cosmopolitan, open-minded, and closer to whiteness.

As a place, I had no direct experience of Kashmir, to the people who live there, or what it feels like to live under occupation. The only access I had was through my grandmother's memories who told us how it was to grow up among the majestic mountains, fragrant forests, and dreamy lakes of her childhood home. She herself was born in Gujranwala, in Punjab, and relocated to Kashmir as a child when her father found employment with the local, then colonial, government. "*Everything and everyone from Kashmir is beautiful,*" she told us, while sadly acknowledging how distant she was now from this magical land and how her grandchildren may never visit because of the violence structuring the state and society. Her life was one of constant change and movement: from Kashmir she relocated to various cities, finally setting up home in Lahore, only to be displaced to Delhi during partition, and then finally in the 1970s joining her son and his family in a suburb of London, UK.

This experience was not specific to my family, it connected us to multiple histories of Kashmiri migratory patterns that have left multiple generations without knowledge of the language or a claim to territory or land. My grandfather's first language was Urdu, and his grandfather's was Farsi. Yet in our present and contemporary condition, our family is unable to contain the fullness of this displacement. Due to these impossibilities, the conditions for demanding loyalties to the Indian state over and above the needs of Kashmiris in Kashmir have flourished and become increasingly dominant. On a personal level, the demand to assert loyalty to the Indian state's claim over Kashmir has been consistent though not always impervious. Against this claim were my grandmother's scattered recollections about the enduring levels of poverty that Muslim Kashmiris endured and that the stark inequalities between Muslims and Hindus made it difficult for her to fully denounce their dissatisfaction with Hindu landowners and regional officials. This doubt was enough of a rupture in my understanding about the violence in Kashmir, so that during much of my childhood I felt confusion and apathy in relation to Kashmiri freedom struggles (Amin & Mushtaq, 2021). Solidarity was always mediated by Brahmin-caste power (Bhan et al., 2020).

The theme of erasure appears and reappears in both state-sanctioned narratives and the intimate family conversations that marked my daily existence. This contributed to a sense of Kashmiri Pandits' existence being much more than simply living; instead, it included the refusal of others' right to life. These ideas connect to a complex decolonial politics of the 1930s and 1940s when demands for independence from British rule crisscrossed with a desire for a strong masculine anti-British leadership that some people found in European fascism. India's anti-colonial movement related to Hitler and Mussolini in ways that are not clear-cut. Anti-colonial factions in India sought out alliances with Italy to plan trade deals when the British left, in other factions freedom fighters drew parallels between European fascism and British imperialism to pronounce a deep paradox in the allies' claim to democracy. A consequence of these politics was the racialization of the Kashmiri Pandit identity that aligned Kashmiri Pandits with Aryans and the place of Kashmir with an Aryan Valley (Bhan et al., 2020). The idea of Kashmiris as pure-blooded and Aryan has perpetuated a politics of violence against Muslims and other minorities in the region, foreclosing non-Hindus' rights to connect to the land and history.

The intersection of Aryan origin stories about the Kashmiri Pandit identity and the family narratives and migratory histories that upturn this purity, enable another way to intervene in practices that reproduce state-sanctioned narratives. However, it is also this intersection that creates ambiguity about what Kashmiri Pandit identity is and as such opens grounds for a protectionist and unitary idea about Indianness. How can we listen to and respond to calls for Azaadi!, for freedom from the Indian occupation of Kashmir when the structures of identity retain a racialized foundation? To open these structures to challenge requires dismantling claims to originary racial lineages and to understand Pandit purity as a false claim. It is from the shifting and collective dimension of memory that we may recover the possibility of solidarity; to respond to the demands for Azaadi by centering safety, life, and sovereignty of all those who live and survive under occupation.

Azaadi

In the sections given earlier we have used our memoryscapes to illustrate how familial narratives interweave with state-sanctioned narratives to manifest particular ideas about Kashmir, Kashmiris, and its struggles. These narratives appear in the everyday and mundane family experiences – appearing as anecdotes, longings, and facts – yet as we have highlighted, these family narratives carry great meaning and political relevance. As post-colonial bodies, we are always at the intersection of a paradox that forgets and recovers a sense of history; we are located between here and the else-where of an occupied Kashmir (Falak, 2020b). By sharing our memory-scapes and placing them side by side, we are able to see how our identities are governed by rules of affect, purity, and erasure; the governance of which is performed by postcolonial bodies.

By placing our memoryscapes in parallel, we notice what is missing, erased, or not known among diverse postcolonial bodies. This in turn shines a light on what we have lost. Our imagination of Kashmir is one that is deracinated from embodied knowing and instead appears as a complexity of violence in which India and Pakistan each absolve themselves of wrong-doing. It is only by bringing these narratives in contact with each other that their claims on Kashmir can be challenged and that our own solidarity with the Kashmiri struggle for freedom better articulated. Falak states, our exist-ence is divided between what really is and what is fetishized in narratives produced by postcolonial states (Falak, 2016a, 2016b).

We have sought to rebuild the ground to establish a dialogue with each other to explicitly call to attention the contradictions and structural para-doxes that shape our lived memories of Kashmiri *azaadi*. By exposing the underbelly of *colonialism otherwise* and the fragments of our differentiated existence, we have tried to recover what the postcolonial state has sought to make us forget. This is where Falak's work guides us in the political acts of memorialization. We read with her to "restore the disrupted itineraries of memory and language without invisibilizing the disruptions and . . . to retrieve the singularity of acts of violence; challenging the state's regulation of affect by producing and circulating an alternate people's affect" (Falak, 2020a, np). We note the overlap and disjuncture in how we imagine violence versus how Falak experiences it. Our memoryscapes portray fleeting and distant fantasies of violence; for Falak this violence is ever-present, it is embodied and structural. Through these conjunctions, we try to absent what our states have deemed to be present and recover what they have deemed to be absent. Instead of imagining Kashmir as paradise, through Falak's work we learn about Kashmir as it is lived, remembered, and experienced every day by Kashmiris who desire freedom. In her juxtaposition of eve-ryday snippets of conversation, dreams, recollections, and prison manuals, we remember what has been absent in our memories; living as if life is con-stantly under siege, where time flow is not measured by days and events but by curfews, where living itself becomes a metaphor of pain (Falak, 2020b).

How can we as postcolonial scholars resist the compulsion to exoticize or empiricize the lived experience of oppression? Our dual memoryscape enables a reading across texts that highlights the importance of positionality while not foreclosing the possibility for complexity. In this way, we mitigate the premise for the postcolonial state to govern the affect, memories, and imaginations that structure collective works of resistance. More importantly, in the act of collective meaning-making, our own desire to show solidarity with "the oppressed" must be critiqued and dissected so that our privilege may be decentered and, in its place, we can identify the conditions for relating to each other differently.

Falak's works show how *Azaadi* is a call to bring body, land, and memory together in ways that manifest wholeness under conditions of violence. Creating connections where loss and erasure have been used by postcolonial states to validate the death of postcolonial others liberate the body from its ethnoreligious superiority. In this way, Azaadi becomes the collective memory which restores a politics of refusal while retaining attention to how difference is mobilized to create hierarchies of life and living.

Concluding Dialogues

Finally, it is important to reflect on what *Azaadi* means for MOS. Decolonizing otherwise, first and foremost, is epistemological, highlighting what Falak (2020a) calls the imaginaries and narratives that are born out of multiple structures of occupation and brutality, but which remain unspeakable in memories and language. It means specifically paying attention to multiple heterogeneities and intersections in which colonialism operates, the spatial encounter between different concepts of the histories, and their power relations. It also means listening to the silences and absences these encounters engender. As Falak (2015b, 2020a, 2020b) notes, today's colonization propagates itself by the regulation of affect, perception management, and stringent control of narrative. It uses the tools of trade developed by management, perpetuates itself in the name of stabilization of economy, opening of new business opportunities, forgetting differences to participate in an unbearably violent orgy of consumption. Decolonial otherwise then seeks to recover and restore the alternative affects, inconsistent narratives, and memories unknown, foregrounding the unspeakability of a limitless war.

Decolonizing otherwise further requires us to be critical of our own position and self-complicity in the business of empire. Modern states produce a rational myth of freedom and emancipation often by providing access to limitless consumption and production. Our autoethnography describes how we live the benefits offered by the nation-state, and that the conditions of our lives make us vulnerable to reproducing state-sanctioned ideas about freedom and security. At the same time, this optimism upholds an irrational myth that ethnocidal genocide and state terror are acceptable prices to pay in exchange for all that a state has to offer. More importantly, we need to be aware of these practices as they operate in postcolonial states, because even in the rudimentary apparatuses for political participation and voicing differences, postcolonial freedom struggles are truncated due to years of colonial onslaught. This creates a naked imperialism that does not require any white man's guilt to justify itself, rather it operates in the name of cultivating a homogenous national identity and the conditions for freedom. Against this backdrop, a radical decolonial praxis requires a dedicated recovery of collective means and sovereign struggles without a common goal. Organizing decoloniality is to work collectively against consensus building, and against what is imaginable or imagined as achievable. This radically different basis of establishing a collective, which we illustrated in our own memoryscapes, is something that is not linear, mapped, bound by time, or even sealed in a single body. Rather it is based on diffused, multilingual, destabilizing dimensions of experience which can challenge the normalization of violence in the name of state-building and capitalism.

References

Ahmad, A. (1997). Post-colonial theory and the post-'condition. *Socialist Register*, *33*, 353–381.

Ahmed, S. (2013). *Strange encounters: Embodied others in post-coloniality*. Routledge.

Akhtar, A. S. (2006). The state as landlord in Pakistani Punjab: Peasant struggles on the Okara military farms. *The Journal of Peasant Studies*, *33*(3), 479–501.

Alcadipani, R., Khan, F. R., Gantman, E., & Nkomo, S. (2012). Southern voices in management and organization knowledge. *Organization*, *19*(2), 131–143.

Anzaldúa, G. (1987). *Borderlands: The new mestiza*. Aunt Lute Books.

Aziz, M. (2007). *Military control in Pakistan: The parallel state*. Routledge.

Bachelard, M. (1998). *The great land grab*. Hyland House.

Banerjee, S. B. (2000). Whose land is it anyway? National interest, indigenous stakeholders, and colonial discourses: The case of the Jabiluka uranium mine. *Organization & Environment*, *13*(1), 3–38.

Banerjee, S. B. (2008). Corporate social responsibility: The good, the bad and the ugly. *Critical Sociology*, *34*(1), 51–79.

Banerjee, S. B., & Linstead, S. (2001). Globalization, multiculturalism and other fictions: Colonialism for the new millennium? *Organization*, *8*(4), 683–722.

Banerjee, S. B., & Osuri, G. (2000). Silences of the media: Whiting out Aboriginality in making news and making history. *Media, Culture & Society*, *22*(3), 263–284.

Bhabha, H. (2015). *Debating cultural hybridity: Multicultural identities and the politics of anti-racism*. Zed Books Ltd.

Bhan, M., & Duschinski, H. (2020). Occupations in context – the cultural logics of occupation, settler violence, and resistance. *Critique of Anthropology*, *40*(3), 285–297.

Bhan, M., Misri, D., & Zia, A. (2020). Relating otherwise: Forging critical solidarities across the Kashmiri pandit-Muslim divide. *Biography, 43*(2), 285–305. doi:10.1353/bio.2020.0030

Chapparban, S. N. (2020). Religious identity and politics of citizenship in South Asia: A reflection on refugees and migrants in India. *Development, 63*(1), 52–59.

Cooke, B. (2003). Managing organizational culture and imperialism. In A. Prasad (Ed.), *Postcolonial theory and organizational analysis: A critical engagement* (pp. 75–94). Palgrave Macmillan.

Cooke, B. (2010). Managerialism as knowing and making in Latin America: International development management and World Bank interventions. In A. Guedes & A. Faria (Eds.), *International management and international relations* (pp. 175–198). Routledge.

Dar, S. (2014). Hybrid accountabilities: When Western and non-Western accountabilities collide. *Human Relations, 67*(2), 131–151.

De Maria, B. (2008). Neo-colonialism through measurement: A critique of the corruption perception index. *Critical Perspectives on International Business, 4*(2/3), 184–202.

Duschinski, H., & Ghosh, S. N. (2017). Constituting the occupation: Preventive detention and permanent emergency in Kashmir. *The Journal of Legal Pluralism and Unofficial Law, 49*(3), 314–337.

Falak, U. (2015a). 13 insomniac moons. *Kindle.* http://kindlemag.in/poems-uzma-falak/

Falak, U. (2015b). Poem: Palestine Kashmir. *The Electronic Intifada.* https://electronicintifada.net/content/poem-palestinekashmir/15016

Falak, U. (2016a). For Mnemosyne. Two poems. *Himal Southasian.* www.himalmag.com/for-mnemosyne/

Falak, U. (2016b). Kashmir: A metaphor of pain Stories through paintings and poetry (part 2). *Himal Southasian.* www.himalmag.com/kashmir-a-metaphor-of-pain/

Falak, U. (2020a). On elsewhereness: Notes from the road, 2016. *Himalaya, the Journal of the Association for Nepal and Himalayan Studies, 40*(1), 13.

Falak, U. (2020b). The smallest unit of time in Kashmir is a siege. *Adi Magazine.* https://adimagazine.com/articles/the-smallest-unit-of-time/

Faria, A. (2013). "Border Thinking in Action: Should Critical Management Studies Get Anything Done?", *Getting Things Done. Dialogues in Critical Management Studies*, Vol. 2, Emerald Group Publishing Limited, Bingley, pp. 277–300. https://doi.org/10.1108/S2046-6072(2013)0000002018

Frenkel, M. (2008). The multinational corporation as a third space: Rethinking international management discourse on knowledge transfer through Homi Bhabha. *Academy of Management Review, 33*(4), 924–942.

Ghosh, S. N., & Duschinski, H. (2020). The grid of indefinite incarceration: Everyday legality and paperwork warfare in Indian-controlled Kashmir. *Critique of Anthropology, 40*(3), 364–384.

Gulrajani, N., & Faure, R. (2019). Donors in transition and the future of development cooperation: What do the data from Brazil, India, China, and South Africa reveal? *Public Administration and Development, 39*(4–5), 231–244.

Ibarra-Colado, E. (2006). Organization studies and epistemic coloniality in Latin America: Thinking otherness from the margins. *Organization, 13*(4), 463–488.

Jack, G., Westwood, R., Srinivas, N., & Sardar, Z. (2011). Deepening, broadening and re-asserting a postcolonial interrogative space in organization studies. *Organization, 18*(3), 275–302.

Kappler, S. (2017). Sarajevo's ambivalent memoryscape: Spatial stories of peace and conflict. *Memory Studies, 10*(2), 130–143. https://doi.org/10.1177/1750698016650484

Kaul, N. (2013, March). The idea of India and Kashmir. *Seminar, 643*, 72–75.

Kazi, S. (2014). Rape, impunity and justice in Kashmir. *Socio-Legal Review, 10*, 14–46.

Khan, F. R., & Lund-Thomsen, P. (2011). CSR as imperialism: Towards a phenomenological approach to CSR in the developing world. *Journal of Change Management, 11*(1), 73–90.

Mandiola, M. P. (2010). Latin America's critical management? A liberation genealogy. *Critical Perspectives on International Business, 6*(2/3), 162–176.

Martinez Dy, A., & Jayawarna, D. (2020). Bios, mythoi and women entrepreneurs: A Wynterian analysis of the intersectional impacts of the COVID-19 pandemic on self-employed women and women-owned businesses. *International Small Business Journal, 38*(5), 391–403.

Masood, A., & Nisar, M. A. (2020). Speaking out: A postcolonial critique of the academic discourse on far-right populism. *Organization, 27*(1), 162–173.

Mignolo, W. D. (2007). Delinking: The rhetoric of modernity, the logic of coloniality and the grammar of de-coloniality. *Cultural Studies, 21*(2–3), 449–514.

Mignolo, W. D. (2011). Geopolitics of sensing and knowing: On (de) coloniality, border thinking and epistemic disobedience. *Postcolonial Studies, 14*(3), 273–283.

Mir, A. (2003). The hegemonic discourse of management texts. *Journal of Management Education, 27*(6), 734–738.

Mir, R., Banerjee, S. B., & Mir, A. (2008). Hegemony and its discontents: A critical analysis of organizational knowledge transfer. *Critical Perspectives on International Business, 4*(2/3), 203–227.

Murphy, E. (2013). Class conflict, state terrorism and the Pakistani military: The Okara military farms dispute. *Critical Studies on Terrorism, 6*(2), 299–311.

Mushtaq, S., & Amin, M. (2021). 'We will memorise our home': exploring settler colonialism as an interpretive framework for Kashmir. *Third World Quarterly, 42*(12), 3012–3029.

Nkomo, S. M. (1992). The emperor has no clothes: Rewriting "race in organizations". *Academy of Management Review, 17*(3), 487–513.

Osuri, G. (2018). Sovereignty, vulnerability, and a gendered resistance in Indian-occupied Kashmir. *Third World Thematics: A TWQ Journal, 3*(2), 228–243.

Osuri, G., & Zia, A. (2020). Kashmir and Palestine: Archives of coloniality and solidarity. *Identities, 27*(3), 249–266.

Prasad, A. (Ed.). (2012). *Against the grain: Advances in postcolonial organization studies* (Vol. 28). Copenhagen Business School Press DK.

Prasad, P., Mills, A. J., Elmes, M. B., & Prasad, A. (1997). *Managing the organizational melting pot: Dilemmas of workplace diversity*. Sage.

Said, E. (1978). *Orientalism: Western concepts of the orient*. Penguin.

Shohat, E. (1992). Third world and post-colonial issues. *Social Text, 31*(32), 99–113. https://doi.org/466220

Srinivas, N. (2009). Against NGOs? A critical perspective on nongovernmental action. *Nonprofit and Voluntary Sector Quarterly, 38*(4), 614–626.

Thompson, L. (2019). Alternative South – South development collaboration? The role of China in the Coega special economic zone in South Africa. *Public Administration and Development, 39*(4–5), 193–202.

Walsh, C. E. (2016). On gender and its 'otherwise'. In W. Harcourt (Ed.), *The Palgrave handbook of gender and development* (pp. 34–47). Palgrave Macmillan.

Yousfi, H. (2014). Rethinking hybridity in postcolonial contexts: What changes and what persists? The Tunisian case of Poulina's managers. *Organization Studies, 35*(3), 393–421.

Yousfi, H. (2021). International management, should we abandon the myth of cultural hybridity? A re-examination of the contribution of postcolonial and decolonial approaches. *M@n@gement, 24*(1), 80–89. www.cairn.info/revue-management-2021-1-page-80.htm

Zia, A. (2019). Blinding Kashmiris: The right to maim and the Indian military occupation in Kashmir. *Interventions, 21*(6), 773–786.

5 Modern Slavery in Contemporary India

Addressing the Elephant in the Room – Contributions From Stringer and Samonova

Swati Nagar

Key Women Academics and Their Contribution to Modern Slavery

This chapter will draw on key women academics and their research on modern slavery. Specifically, the chapter draws on Christina Stringer and Elena Samonova. The chapter encompasses key themes from their work and examines modern slavery in contemporary India. Although Stringer and Samanova are not of South Asian origin, they make a vital contribution to exploring the nature and extent of modern slavery in the South Asian context. Their research primarily discusses the nature of slavery, labor exploitation and its implications for both business and society. It is important to note that the chapter only addresses some of the leading works of these academics. This chapter contributes by extending and adjusting Stringer and Samanova's theoretical apparatus to understand modern slavery in the context of India.

The first academic addressed in this chapter is Christina Stringer (Associate Professor, University of Auckland, New Zealand). Her work sits directly on the cross-over between academic research and advocacy for a better community. Christina has made critical contributions in examining the extent of labor exploitation in South Asia (University of Auckland, 2020).

More recently, Stringer's work through a case study of Asia-Pacific investigates forced and IUU labor practices on distant waters fishing vessels in the Asia-Pacific (Yea & Stringer, 2021). The authors argue that identifying the dynamics of the interconnections between forced and IUU labor practices necessitates a more detailed examination of both approaches at the scale of individual fishing vessels and crew. One of the conceptual contributions of this study is that it examines the reasons trafficked fishers engage in IUU fishing practices. Also, a twofold characterization of exploitation involving the two interlinked aspects of "labor" and "situation" frames the

DOI: 10.4324/9781003197270-7

analysis (Yea & Stringer, 2021). Similarly, Stinger's article, "Under the shadow: Forced labor among sea fishers in Thailand" discusses the widespread exploitation of workers in the Thai fishing industry (Chantavanicha et al., 2016). She presents essential insights into deceptive and coercive recruitment practices, exploitative working conditions, and forced labor in the fishing industry (Chantavanicha et al., 2016). Stringer has also examined the nature and extent of modern slavery in global value chains (GVCs) in South Asia's apparel industry (Stringer & Michailova, 2018b). In particular, her work explores why slavery exists in GVCs and what this means for multinational enterprises (MNEs). She also considers how better governance of GVCs can protect the workers' rights and prevent exploitation. She responds to two critical arguments by Buckley and Ghauri's (2004) and Lee and Gereffi (2015) on the need to incorporate the social impact of labor exploitation in the broader international business and organizational studies literature (Khattak et al., 2017; Islam & Stringer, 2018). Presenting data from five supplier firms in Bangladesh and Sri Lanka, their work makes a considerable conceptual contribution to how better governance of GVCs can prevent mental and physical abuse and protect the rights of those employed in the apparel industry. This research adds to emerging literature seeking to integrate the mainstream GVC literature by providing insight into an under-theorized aspect – the relationship between the governance of GVCs and modern slavery (Khattak et al., 2017; Islam & Stringer, 2018).

Stringer has also called upon a further academic discussion on how modern slavery is linked to the business. In particular, her contributions present an insight into how globally disaggregated production systems governed through ownership and contracts by MNEs are one of the leading causes of labor exploitation. Her work notes that numerous mechanisms and practices mask the presence of modern slavery across the globe. Her research states that uncovering modern slavery is a grand challenge that can and should be tackled by researchers and educators (Burmester et al., 2019; Michailova et al., 2020).

The second academic addressed in this chapter is Elena Samonova (Post-doctoral fellow at University College Dublin, Ireland). Her work examines the most pervasive forms of modern slavery: bonded labor in Nepal and India. Bonded labor is linked with a credit agreement, leaving a debtor bound to repay their debt through long-term servitude (Samonova, 2019). Contributing to the literature on the human rights-based approach, she interprets slavery as a violation of human rights and focuses on the empowerment of slaves as rights holders. Her work contributes to modern slavery literature by explicitly exploring the links between rights, power inequality, and oppression. By identifying the factors and forces that contribute to and reinforce bonded labor situation in South Asia, her work demonstrates how bonded labor is connected to colonization, dispossession, and migration (Samonova, 2019).

The extensive research into an unpalatable part of the economy and society has established these academics as international experts on different aspects of modern slavery. Their work is pivotal in understanding the concept of modern slavery and the need for corrective action by businesses, the government, and society to stop such exploitative practices. A standard view demonstrated by their work is that academics have a strong responsibility to examine and address urgent social issues is a much-needed perspective in business and organizational studies today. The following section outlines the concept of Modern slavery and its prevalence in India.

Modern Slavery

Slavery is considered mainly a historical phenomenon. However, the enslavement of vulnerable individuals is a reality even today (Global Slavery Index, 2018). The contemporary version of this social stain ranges from pauper's wages to forced labor. Modern slavery keeps workers in an abusive employment arrangement. It has become a pervasive and insidious part of the global economy, moving from child labor in developing nations to migrant workers facing illegal and cruel work practices in the middle of the developed world's metropolises (Hodal, 2019).

While modern slavery is a global issue, it is more widespread in developing economies. Rapid economic globalization has given rise to production hubs in densely populated countries (e.g., India and China). This has created "disposable people," often in millions, rendered unfree by the final authority of violence (Bales, 2012, p. 5). Modern slavery is a broad term that comprises activities including bonded and forced labor, human trafficking, and other forms of commercial exploitation (Crane, 2013; Stringer & Michailova, 2018a; Samonova, 2019). Although the term "Modern slavery" lacks a legal definition, in recent years it has gained considerable currency as a term encompassing forced labor, human trafficking, slavery, and other forms of exploitation (Stringer & Michailova, 2018a). It is characterized by violence, restriction of personal freedom, and a high level of exploitation and it no longer involves the formal legal designation of persons as chattels (Hodal, 2019). Still, as noted by Stringer and Samonova, workers in various industries find themselves subject to complete control of their employers. In other words, employers employ a range of practices to exercise the right to ownership. These workers are worked until they cannot continue and are discarded (Hewamanne, 2019; Samonova, 2019; Stringer & Michailova, 2018a). Also, as these workers mostly come from impoverished socioeconomic backgrounds and are often uneducated, they are more vulnerable to physical and physiological abuse (Hewamanne, 2020; Hodal, 2019; Stringer & Michailova, 2018a).

Though modern slavery is present in all countries, the most significant proportion of it, approximately 64 per cent, is employed in forced labor situations in developing countries in the Asia-Pacific region (ILO, 2017). This region is important to multinational enterprises (MNE), and by extension, to business and organization studies scholars. Today, an estimated 40.3 million people – more than three times the figure during the transatlantic slave trade – live in some form of modern slavery (ILO, 2017). Women and girls comprise 71 per cent of all modern slavery victims. Children make up 25 per cent and account for 10 million of all the slaves worldwide (ILO, 2017).

Modern Slavery in India

In the Americas, slavery resulted from the international slave trade, where slaves were brought to American shores to work in agriculture, construction, manufacturing, and domestic service. However, in India, the slavery of certain groups was internal and often based on caste and social status. Although slavery was formally abolished in India in 1843 by the East India Company (pre-independence), it contributed to the transformation of the traditional concept of slavery resulting in bonded labor (debt bondage) (Major, 2012). By the middle of the nineteenth century, debt bondage became a technically acceptable way to secure de facto slave labor. Indeed, it became the primary mode of existing slavery across the whole Indian subcontinent (Samonova, 2019).

Several forms of forced and bonded labor concerning debt came into existence during India's colonial period and have continued to prevail in today's contemporary Indian society. The Global Slavery Index estimates that on any given day in 2016, nearly 8 million people were living in modern slavery in India. This means that are approximately 6.1 victims for every thousand people. However, other estimates from the Global Slavery Index (2018) suggest 18.3 million people in modern slavery in India. The difference reflects changes in counting rules and estimation methods (Global Slavery Index, 2018b). Bonded labor is increasingly found in urban industries, which in many ways is a result of economic liberalization and increased outsourcing of production to cost-effective destinations like India (Samonova, 2019). Even though generational and family bonded labor has decreased, new forms of bonded labor have emerged. Bonded labor exists predominantly in the informal and unregulated sectors, and a vast majority of those employed come from impoverished socioeconomic backgrounds (Molchanova, 2019; Samonova, 2019).

While much of Stringer's published work examines migrant exploitation in New Zealand, many of her articles can be used as a lens to understand the atrocities against vulnerable workers in India. For example, her paper on the Thai fishing industry can be applied to examine the exploitation of migrant workers in the Indian fishing industry (Chantavanicha et al., 2016). Like Thailand, India's fishing industry is a leading revenue earner for several coastal regions (Alex, 2019). Most fisheries in India are small-medium businesses that fish primarily within domestic shores (World Fishing & Aquaculture, 2020). Lack of infrastructure, technology, and reliance on traditional fishing methods often mean that most fisheries tend to have low-value catches (revenue). Traditional fishing methods with limited capital make it difficult to ensure fair working conditions onboard their vessels (World Fishing & Aquaculture, 2020). For example, most industry workers rely on daily wages, which makes them dependent on their employers. In some cases, these workers are also sources of bonded labor aboard foreign-flagged vessels that fish in their waters. While the Indian government has promised assistance to help the industry and its workers, the measures provide little support and protection to the most vulnerable (Global Slavery Index, 2018a).

Similarly, research by Stringer on the nature and extent of modern slavery in GVCs and global factory is very relevant when analyzing the exploitation of workers in the Indian apparel industry. Low wages and weak labor laws have long made India attractive for foreign brands that outsource work. The industry employs over 12.9 million people in factories and millions more outside, including their own homes (Vaidyanathan, 2020). Unions are virtually absent in the private sector, making informal and contract workers especially vulnerable. Workers often work long hours (typically 10–12 hours) in an environment of fear and abuse (Vaidyanathan, 2020). Although inspections are mandatory, rampant corruption and a sluggish system have meant that factories rarely account for breaking the law. Advocates of fair working conditions in India state it is the responsibility of brands to ensure appropriate and safe working conditions (Vaidyanathan, 2020). Stringer supports this view. Her work on labor exploitation states that MNEs and their contractors play a critical role in advocating and protecting workers' rights (Hewamanne, 2020; Khattak et al., 2017; Islam et al., 2017; Islam & Stringer, 2018). Having discussed the relationship between outsourcing and modern slavery; the following section considers the implications of social discrimination and Modern slavery.

Role of Social Discrimination in Modern Slavery

Embedded in Hinduism, the purpose of the caste system was to divide the society and its population into four distinct groups. Each social group served a purpose in contributing to the economy and welfare of society. A hierarchy of work that was once traditionally determined by caste to develop a thriving community has transformed itself into a pervasive social system (Alex, 2019; Samonova, 2019). In contemporary India, this system has failed to provide equal opportunity for development and prosperity to the most underprivileged social groups – Other Backward Class (OBC), Schedule Caste (SC), and Schedule Tribes (ST) (Alex, 2019). The outcome of this inequality is poverty and prejudice, which exacerbates the vulnerability of the aforementioned ostracized social groups (Alex, 2019). As of 2019, OBC accounted for more than 40 per cent of the Indian population, while ST and SC formed less than ten per cent of the total population (Statista, 2020). These groups often viewed to be at the bottom or on the social hierarchy periphery and are not allowed to work in roles deemed for the high castes (Alex, 2019). Derogatory terms such as "untouchable," among others, are frequently applied to describe these communities. This notion also implies that they have an "untouchable" area of work, in most places, limiting their access to economic opportunities. These communities are often degraded, humiliated, and expected to be docile to high caste (Alex, 2019; Upadhyaya, 2017). These caste rules are enforced by the threat of adverse consequences if they are opposed. If these marginalized groups defy traditional exploitative, discriminatory, and humiliating roles, they face social sanctions and boycotts. This further restricts any opportunity to overcome discrimination, discrimination-related poverty, and dependency on their employers or landlords (Alex, 2019; Upadhyaya, 2017).

As evident from the work of Stringer and Samonova, modern slavery thrives at the conjunction of poverty and discrimination. Given the extent of discrimination and social deprivation that OBC, SC, and ST groups face, they are more susceptible to modern slavery. Desperate for work, workers from these marginalized racial and minority groups are often employed in high-risk industries. These industries may include (but are not limited to) transport, cleaning, brick kilns, scrape and metal, construction, local roadside restaurants/cafes, domestic work, mining, and manufacturing. In certain instances, people are born into "hereditary" slavery if their mother or father was a slave (Samonova, 2019). This exploitative practice is observed in the agriculture sector, where workers are bonded to the landlords. As workers from these communities travel to other destinations for work, they can often face heightened vulnerability to bondage and exploitation due to unfamiliar surroundings (International Dalit Solidarity Network, 2020a). Lack of social networks, language barriers, and tight surveillance makes these workers more exposed to exploitation. For instance, workers from the Kokrajhar district of Assam employed in brick kilns in Punjab often live in isolated locations, have limited connections to the local community, and have little social support in emergencies. In such instances, workers are entirely reliant on their employers, who often restrict their movement (Upadhyaya, 2017).

Further, the lack of adequate safety equipment, training, and measures means that these workers are particularly exposed to higher occupational risks. This, combined with a lack of awareness of their rights, makes this group of workers particularly vulnerable to exploitation and prone to debt bondage and other forms of forced labor (International Dalit Solidarity Network, 2020a, 2020b). More recently, the pandemic has added to the woes of these communities. More than 100 million internal migrant workers were forced to return home due to the nationwide lockdown in 2020. Many of these workers have no social protection schemes and earn daily wages. Also, marginalized communities often suffer discrimination in access to resources and relief. If these workers were to get sick, there is no social safety net to prevent them from falling deeper into poverty. Indeed, the pandemic is expected to reinforce inequality and further push these communities into greater poverty and deprivation (International Dalit Solidarity Network, 2020b).

It is important to note that differing perspectives examine the plight of the most vulnerable in the South Asian context. For example, Samonova (2019) addresses the relationship between caste and the extent of exploitation. In comparison, Stringer does not address modern slavery based on caste. Her work examines the relationship between socioeconomic class and modern slavery. For example, her work on the fishing and apparel industries highlights the relationship between socioeconomic status and exploitation. These research projects also emphasize that social deprivation is the fundamental cause of labor abuse. Similarly, her work also states that temporary migrant workers, regardless of their country/social background, are more prone to exploitation as they rely on their employers. It is also important to note that her research delineates that modern slavery exists in developed and developing economies. To this end, the different perspectives on modern slavery in South Asia suggest that exploitation is not always related to or based on one's caste or religion. Instead, in a postcolonial context, modern slavery results from opportunistic firm behavior.

The Feminization of Modern Slavery

Feminist thinkers have attempted to assess the relationship between economic development and the liberalization of women (Federici, 1975; Mies, 1986; Saffioti, 1978). Several researchers argue that economic growth, especially in postcolonial countries like India, has not translated into women's liberation (Sen & Grown, 1987). They suggest that while economic development has led to a significant number of employment opportunities for women, it has also led to greater exploitation of women. This is especially true for women that belong to lower social groups. Other feminist anthropologists have argued that women's role in the labor market is key to understanding women's social status and power in a given society (Samonova, 2019). To theorize the problematic relation of women to social class, Ferguson (1979) argues that at least three different variables – an individual's work, the family of origin, and present household economic unit – relate to an individual's social class and economic power. Alex (2019) supports this view and states that women from socially deprived backgrounds in India are bonded in their own right. Women from marginalized communities often struggle with property inheritance discrimination and face restrictions on movement and primary education. In addition to employment, women are burdened by unpaid work within the family. This work is unrecognized because it is not tied to income. This lack of recognition is mirrored in the workplace.

The entry of women into the lower strata of the social and economic hierarchy has significantly increased in India, especially in the last two decades (Alex, 2019). In many cases, this happens; when the primary male earner loses employment (due to either their age or downsizing because of technological change), women have to work to fulfill the family's needs (Desai, 2020). Despondent for work, women seek employment in small-scale industries (the unorganized sector) such as bangle production, carpet making, apparel manufacturing, fish-processing, silk farming, tea and coffee plantations, quarries, apparel and weaving, and domestic work (Choi-Fitzpatrick, 2017; Hewamanne, 2020; Nagaraj, 2020). Women in these industries are more exposed to exploitative working conditions. Also, as most women are illiterate and unaware of their rights, it worsens their plight (Hewamanne, 2020). Indeed, studies on the exploitation of women in India suggest that illiteracy is more common among women than men. For example, according to research conducted by Desai (2020), seven out of every ten women workers employed in the unorganized sector only complete their primary schooling. The proportion among males in a similar category is 37 per cent. The ratio of illiterates is also comparatively lower among men. Poor economic and social conditions often mean that most women cannot pursue education beyond a certain level. They are far more critical as wage-earners as they contribute to the family's income at an early age. Financial costs and cultural views often discourage parents from educating their daughters. According to Desai (2020), OBCs, intermediate castes, and religious minorities (e.g., Muslims) are the three largest groups of women workers employed in the unorganized sector. The research further states that nine out of ten women workers are typically aged between 14 and 40 years. Breman (1996) confirms this in her work on the informal economy in India. Taking an example from the textile industry, she notes that only one in ten power loom operators is older than 40 – "*the labour process is so exhausting that very few can perform adequately after middle age*" (Breman, 1996, p. 61).

In addition to academic research, numerous media inquiries on modern slavery validate the predicament of women workers in the Indian apparel industry. For example, an investigative report by Vaidyanathan for the BBC states that women workers in Indian factories supplying the supermarket chains Marks & Spencer, Tesco and Sainsbury's, and the fashion brand Ralph Lauren are subjected to exploitative conditions (Vaidyanathan, 2020). Women working at a Ralph Lauren supplier are often forced to stay overnight to complete orders, sometimes requiring them to sleep on the factory floor. They are also refused lunch and bathroom breaks and prevented from going home until they finish their work. The women also reported being constantly threatened by the employers that they might risk losing their jobs should they fail to comply with their demands. They often do not receive equal remuneration for equal work and face harassment and abuse in the workplace. The women working at these garment factories all live in poverty, and many belong to the OBC group. Even though the Indian government has various labor laws to protect women, these have little impact in reality. For example, the Factories Act (1948) states that no worker should exceed more than 48 hours a week (or 60 hours with overtime), nor should they be made to work for more than nine hours in one day. Regardless of their gender, workers are entitled to fair wages and working conditions. The law also states that women should only work night shifts if they choose to do so (Labour Commissioner, 2019). However, the working conditions and the nature and extent of exploitation discussed in the above example suggest that the laws have little impact on protecting the most vulnerable. Indeed, the combined effects of low education levels, workplace discrimination, and a lack of economic freedom increase women's vulnerability to labor exploitation and dependency (Hewamanne, 2020). The phenomenon of women increasingly being bonded in a free labor market can be referred to as the "feminisation of modern slavery."

Government and Industry Response to Modern Slavery

The Government of India has criminalized most forms of modern slavery, including trafficking, slavery, forced and bonded labor, and child sexual exploitation. Over the decades, there has been significant progress in national legislation to incorporate numerous activities classified as modern slavery. For example, the trafficking of Persons (Prevention, Protection and

Rehabilitation) Bill was approved in March 2018 (Ministry of Labour & Employment, 2016). This bill called for creating a separate agency dedicated to investigating trafficking crimes. It proposed establishing anti-trafficking committees and special courts at district, state, and central government to prosecute trafficking crimes. It also included provisions for cross-border repatriation of victims from neighboring countries. The bill called for greater monitoring of employment agencies involved in exploiting migrant workers through forced labor (Pandit, 2020).

Similarly, the domestic workers' national platform submitted a draft of the – domestic workers regulation of work and social security bill – in 2017. This bill seeks to extend existing labor laws to cover domestic workers and ensure they are entitled to minimum wage and social security. However, the process of formulating a national policy is still in the "draft stage" (Global Slavery Index, 2018b; Sampath, 2017).

The government established the "central sector scheme for rehabilitation of bonded labor" in 2016. This scheme recognizes the needs of different groups trapped in bonded labor. It offers them monetary compensation of approximately US$1,379 to male bonded laborers and US$2,758 to women and children trapped in bonded labor (Ministry of Labour & Employment, 2016; Somasekarappa, 2019). This bill has played a vital role in helping the most vulnerable by compensating them for rebuilding their lives. However, there is still work to do in recovery and successful rehabilitation, which requires a much broader range of support services and assistance. The government runs two schemes to rehabilitate women and children subject to modern slavery – *Ujjawala* and *Swadhar Greh*. These schemes initiated by the Ministry of Women and Child Development offer shelter and rehabilitation services for rescued women and children. The *Ujjawala* scheme is specifically for female victims of trafficking. In contrast, the *Swadhar Greh* program provides support services for victims of domestic violence, homeless women, and women in distress who need shelter. The Ministry also runs campaigns to promote awareness of its services in the local communities (Government of India, 2018; Ministry of Women and Child Development, 2016). While these schemes are a step in the right direction, the fragmented nature of the industry that attracts such labor makes it challenging for government provisions to reach the most vulnerable.

From an industry perspective, the 2013 Companies Act, for example, requires medium to large-sized firms to spend two per cent of their three-year annual average net profit on Corporate Social Responsibility (CSR) activities. Initiatives may include poverty reduction, education, health, environmental sustainability, gender equality, and vocational skills development (Global Slavery Index, 2018b). The act also requires firms to establish a CSR committee and submit an annual report on their

CSR activities. However, it does not explicitly need firms to spend this allocated money on modern slavery initiatives. While the act is a positive step forward, it has limited impact. For example, anecdotal evidence suggests that some firms that previously spent more on CSR activities had scaled their spending down to the mandated two per cent. This may be because the requirements are seen more as legal compliance than a firm's reputation building or branding exercise (Global Slavery Index, 2018b).

Similarly, the National Voluntary Guidelines framework has led to the development of the Responsible Business Index. The index analyzes the policies, disclosures, and mechanisms of the top 100 firms listed on the Bombay Stock Exchange. The index ranks the top 100 firms on their performance on five parameters – inclusive supply chain, community as stakeholders, community development, employee dignity and human rights, and non-discrimination at the workplace (Agarwal, 2018). Although there are some improvements, only 77 (of the total 100) have committed to inclusive supply chains (Global Slavery Index, 2018b).

While current legislation and schemes have made provisions to recover and rehabilitate workers from modern slavery, further work is needed in the legislative space to ensure that firms are held accountable for their actions. As the global movement against human trafficking has gained traction, many governments and organizations promised far-reaching steps to eradicate the problem. For example, in 2015, the UK government established the Modern Slavery Act, which seeks to prevent and prosecute modern slavery (Hewamanne, 2020). Article 54 of the act, dealing with transparency in supply chains, requires due diligence from British companies to manage human trafficking within their global supply chains (Hewamanne, 2020). Australia also founded the Modern Slavery Act in 2018. This Act requires firms (based or operating in Australia) with annual revenue of more than AUD100 million to report on the risks of modern slavery in their operations and supply chains and actions to address those risks (Federal Register of Legislation, 2018). Similarly, to better address the issue, the Government of India could also consider establishing a Modern Slavery Act. The purpose of this Act could be to require due diligence from firms based and operating in India (both domestic and foreign). In doing so, the government could better manage the risks of slavery and protect the most vulnerable in the communities. Also, together with the existing provisions, such an Act would perhaps help better tackle the contentious issue at the grassroots level in India.

Response from Academia – Are We Doing Enough?

As academics, we are mindful of institutional and industry calls to ensure our students understand and are prepared to respond to ethical issues that are particularly prevalent in business today. These calls are not new, starting with concerns around sweatshop practices during the 1990s and heightened with calls for a paradigm shift in business studies dating back to a decade ago (Holland, 2009). We often employ a "learning by doing" strategy in our courses to encourage deep learning. This is achieved by engaging both theoretical and applied content, especially when addressing corporate social responsibility, ethical conduct, labor abuse and exploitation, and the role of gender or caste. Although these topics feature in the business curricula, the availability of data is an issue. For example, disciplines of organizational behavior, supply chain management, and ethics often have a range of case-based examples and journal and editorial articles that discuss such aspects. However, it is often challenging to apply the literature from those sources to a traditional business classroom. This paucity of materials is perhaps because the frameworks and the mainstream literature do not sufficiently address the "dark side" of globalization.

The limited availability of mainstream academic research and teaching resources means that academics often use examples covered in the media. The nature of the material in the media also means that class debates on how the need and desire to achieve the triple bottom line relate to firm strategy and the broader social and institutional environment, potentially the driving force behind modern slavery, remain primarily superficial. From a pedagogical perspective, the scarcity of academic research and teaching resources on such topics makes it challenging to create awareness and much-needed critical reasoning skills among the business student body.

Stringer echoes the need for more significant discussion and debate on the issue of modern slavery. Her article, *Tackling Modern Slavery, the Ugliest Phenomenon of Our Times: An Invitation to the IB Scholarly Community* (Stringer & Michailova, 2018a), calls for greater attention and discussion on modern slavery within the academic community. She states that while academics are aware of the issue, mainstream research remains largely silent on the topic of modern slavery and the reasons behind it. Recognizing this need, she has since co-edited an AIB insights special issue on "Investigating Modern Slavery: How IB Scholarship Can Contribute" (2020). The special issue was devoted to different aspects of modern slavery and how academic research can better address the phenomenon.

Our article in the AIB Insights special issue – "*Investigating Modern Slavery: How IB Scholarship Can Contribute*" (August 2020) – outlines the need for greater academic interaction on the topic of modern slavery. In this article, I, together with my co-author (Fiona Hurd), call for creating a wider variety of accessible teaching material and experiential activities that can be employed in the business classroom to encourage analysis of modern slavery and related crimes. For this, we propose a collective repository developed by academics. The purpose would be to host a collection of teaching material, cases, media articles, industry, and government reports that specifically address the topic of modern slavery from a business, social, and institutional viewpoint. Such a repository, in our view, can be made available to all academics interested in modern slavery. The repository can be made available on various academic platforms (e.g., leading conferences landing pages). The aim is to invite academics from multiple disciplines to contribute and access teaching resources as required. The purpose of the repository would be to facilitate more significant interaction and dialogue both in the classroom and amongst fellow academics (Nagar & Hurd, 2020).

Moreover, by embedding such approaches in mainstream literature, we position such issues as central to business activities. We also call for the development of new courses in the wider business curricula. Little acknowledgment of modern slavery from a critical perspective makes it difficult for the business faculty to challenge students' preconceptions of slavery as a historical phenomenon. Considering this, it is vital that academics connect (via a common platform linked to the repository) to exchange ideas for new courses and topics that address modern slavery as a critical phenomenon.

Conclusion

This chapter addresses the critical issue of modern slavery. While forms of contemporary slavery widely exist across several spheres, academic research on this topic (especially in India) is relatively limited. The chapter aims to contribute to the existing literature gap. Building on Stringer and Samanova's work, the chapter outlined the nature of modern slavery prevalent in India. In particular, it discussed the most pervasive forms of modern slavery – bonded labor. The chapter identified the main driving forces behind bonded labor and examined the link between poverty, social discrimination, and bonded labor. Removing caste-based stigma is, therefore, imperative to eliminating bondage. Also, the feminization of modern slavery is a less explored phenomenon. Approximately 71 per cent of labor subject to modern slavery are women and girls. Yet, there is limited academic research that examines the fundamental reasons behind the exploitation of women, especially in India. The chapter concludes with an outline of government schemes and policies currently in place to protect the most vulnerable. While government action has seen success in the recovery and rehabilitation of victims of modern slavery, further work is required to address this issue in India. Similarly, academics specializing in modern slavery have the responsibility of furthering discussions on this critical matter and should be conscientious about incorporating research into mainstream business and organizational studies literature.

References

Agarwal, N. (2018). Measuring business responsibility disclosures of Indian companies: A data-driven approach to influence action. *Business and Human Rights*, *3*(1), 123–129. https://doi.org/10.1017/bhj.2017.27

Alex, D. R. (2019). Woman as honor, man as reformer: Transition of women's work roles in the Hindu fishing caste of Kerala, India. *Women's Studies – An Interdisciplinary Journal*, *48*, 862–881. https://doi.org/10.1080/00497878.2019.1676744

Bales, K. (2012). *Disposable people – New slavery in the global economy* (Vol. 3rd, 336 pp). University of California Press.

Breman, J. (1996). *Footloose labour – working in India's informal economy* (278 pp). Cambridge University Press.

Buckley, P., & Ghauri, P. (2004). Globalisation, Economic Geography and the Strategy of Multinational Enterprises. *Journal of International Business Studies*, *35*, 81–98.

Burmester, B., Michailova, S., & Stringer, C. (2019). Modern slavery and international business scholarship: The governance nexus. *Critical Perspectives on International Business*, *15*. https://doi.org/10.1108/cpoib-02-2019-0011

Chantavanicha, S., Laodumrongchaia, S., & Stringer, C. (2016). Under the shadow: Forced labour among sea fishers in Thailand. *Marine Policy*, *68*, 1–7. https://doi.org/10.1016/j.marpol.2015.12.015

Choi-Fitzpatrick, A. (2017, April 28). Cruelty or keeping it in the family? What I learned from India's slaveholders. *The Guardian*. Retrieved February 2, 2020, from www.theguardian.com/global-development/2017/apr/28/what-i-learned-from-india-slaveowners-austin-choi-fitzpatrick

Crane, A. (2013). Modern slavery as a management practice: Exploring the conditions and capabilities for human exploitation. *Academy of Management Journal*, *38*(1), 49–69. http://dx.doi.org/10.5465/amr.2011.0145

Desai, K. (2020). Exploitation and liberation: Case study of women workers in Surat's unorganised sector. *Social Change*, *50*(1), 12–27. https://doi.org/10.1177/0049085719901051

Federici, S. (1975). *Wages against housework*. New Clarion Press.

Federal Register of Legislation. (2018). *Modern slavery act 2018*. Retrieved December 18, 2021, from www.legislation.gov.au/Details/C2018A00153

Ferguson, A. (1979). *Women as a new revolutionary class in the US* (pp. 279–304). Southend Press.

Global Slavery Index. (2018a). *Fishing*. Retrieved February 25, 2021, from www.globalslaveryindex.org/2018/findings/importing-risk/fishing/

Global Slavery Index. (2018b). *INDIA*. Retrieved November 20, 2020, from www.globalslaveryindex.org/2018/findings/country-studies/india/

Government of India. (2018). *Swadhar Greh scheme*. Retrieved March 5, 2021, from www.india.gov.in/spotlight/swadhar-greh-scheme

Hewamanne, S. (2020). Surveillance by another name: The modern slavery act, global factory workers, and part-time sex work in Sri Lanka. *Journal of Women in Culture & Society*, *45*, 653–677. https://doi.org/10.1086/706471

Hodal, K. (2019). One in 200 people is a slave. Why? *The Guardian*. Retrieved January 5, 2020, from www.theguardian.com/news/2019/feb/25/modern-slavery-trafficking-persons-one-in-200

Holland, H. (2009). Is it time to retrain B-schools? *New York Times*. Retrieved October 29, 2019, from www.nytimes.com/2009/03/15/business/15school.html

ILO. (2017). Global estimates of modern slavery: Forced labour and forced marriage. Retrieved October 17, 2019, www.ilo.org/wcmsp5/groups/public/–dgreports/dcomm/documents/publications/wcms_5 75479.pdf

International Dalit Solidarity Network. (2020a). *UN experts raise concern over caste-based slavery*. Retrieved February 2, 2021, from https://idsn.org/un-experts-raise-concern-over-caste-based-slavery/

International Dalit Solidarity Network. (2020b). *Vulnerable workers in supply chains need urgent protection to survive impact of Covid-19*. Retrieved February 2, 2021, from https://idsn.org/vulnerable-workers-in-supply-chains-need-urgent-protection-to-survive-impact-of-covid-19/

Islam, T., Khattak, A., & Stringer, C. (2017). A governance deficit in the apparel industry in Bangladesh: Solutions to the impasse? In *Governing corporate social responsibility in the apparel industry after Rana Plaza* (pp. 111–145). Palgrave Macmillan.

Islam, T., & Stringer, C. (2018). Challenges of achieving social upgrading in Bangladesh's apparel industry. *Society and Business Review*, *15*. https://doi.org/10.1108/SBR-07-2018-0068

Khattak, A., Stringer, C., Haworth, N., & Benson-Rea, M. (2017). Is social upgrading occurring in South Asia's apparel industry? *Critical Perspectives on International Business*, *13*(3), 226–243. https://doi.org/10.1108/cpoib-11-2015-0051

Labour Commissioner. (2019). *The Factories Act, 1948*. Retrieved March 3, 2021, from https://labour.delhi.gov.in/content/factories-act-1948-0

Lee, J., & Gereffi, G. (2015). Global Value Chains, Rising Power Firms and Economic and Social Upgrading. *Critical Perspectives on International Business*, *11*, 319–339.

Major, A. (2012). *Slavery, abolitionism and empire in India, 1772–1843* (Vol. 6, p. 385). Liverpool University Press.

Mies, M. (1986). *Patriarchy and accumulation on a world scale: Women in the international division of labour* (p. 251). Zed Books.

Ministry of Labour and Employment. (2016). *Central sector scheme for rehabilitation of bonded labourer*. Ministry of Labour & Employment. Retrieved February 2, 2021, from https://labour.gov.in/sites/default/files/OM_CSS_Rehab_BL_2016_1.pdf

Ministry of Women and Child Development. (2016). *UJJAWALA: A comprehensive scheme for prevention of trafficking and rescue, rehabilitation and re-integration of victims of trafficking and commercial sexual exploitation*. Government of

India. Retrieved February 2, 2021, from https://wcd.nic.in/sites/default/files/Ujjawala%20New%20Scheme.pdf

Michailova, S., Stringer, C., & Mezias, J. (2020). Letter from the editors: Special issue on "Investigating modern slavery: How IB scholarship can contribute". *AIB Insights*. https://doi.org/ 10.46697/001c.14362

Molchanova, V. S. (2019). Modern slavery in India: The essence, forms, distribution. *Slavery: Theory and Practice*, *4*(1), 20–28. https://doi.org/10.13187/slave.2019.1.20

Nagar, S., & Hurd, F. (2020). Addressing modern slavery in the IB classroom: Are we doing enough? *AIB Insights*, *20*(2). https://doi.org/https://doi.org/10.46697/001c.13543

Nagaraj, A. (2020, January 9). *Indian slavery survivors swap life of bondage for seat in boardroom at tea plantation*. Retrieved March 5, 2021, from https://news.trust.org/item/20200109095732-0rc77

Pandit, A. (2020). Reporting of crime a must in new anti-trafficking bill. *The Times of India*. Retrieved September 3, 2021, from https://timesofindia.indiatimes.com/india/reporting-of-crime-a-must-in-new-anti-trafficking-bill/articleshow/74644233.cms

Saffioti, H. (1978). *Women in class society* (178 pp). Monthly Review Press.

Samonova, E. (2019). *Modern slavery and bonded labour in South Asia – a human rights-based approach* (318 pp). Routledge.

Sampath, G. (2017, July 14). It's not help, it's work. *The Hindu*. Retrieved August 9, 2020, from www.thehindu.com/opinion/op-ed/its-not-help-its-work/article19273135.ece

Sen, G., & Grown, C. (1987). *Development, crises and alternative visions: Third world perspectives* (128 pp). Monthly Review Press.

Somasekarappa, G. (2019). *Legal guide – identification, rescue, rehabilitation and prosecution of bonded labour in the brick kiln industry*. Anti-Slavery International. www.antislavery.org/wp-content/uploads/2019/12/Legal-Guide-bonded-labour-India-brick-kiln.pdf

Statista Research Department. (2020). *Share of caste demographics India 2019*. Retrieved January 21, 2021, from www.statista.com/statistics/1001016/india-population-share-by-caste/

Stringer, C., & Michailova, S. (2018a). Tackling modern slavery, the ugliest phenomenon of our times: An invitation to the IB scholarly community. *AIB Insights*, *18*(2), 4. https://doi.org/10.46697/001c.16840

Stringer, C., & Michailova, S. (2018b). Why modern slavery thrives in multinational corporations' global value chains. *Multinational Business Review*, *26*. https://doi.org/10.1108/MBR-04-2018-0032

University of Auckland. (2020). *Associate Professor Christina Anne Stringer*. Retrieved February 25, 2020, from www.business.auckland.ac.nz/people/cstr020

Upadhyaya, K. P. (2017). *Poverty, discrimination and slavery – the reality of bonded labour in India, Nepal and Pakistan*. Anti-Slavery International. www.antislavery.org/wp-content/uploads/2017/01/1-poverty-discrimination-slavery-final.pdf

Vaidyanathan, R. (2020). Indian factory workers supplying major brands allege routine exploitation. *BBC*. www.bbc.com/news/world-asia-54960346

World Fishing & Aquaculture. (2020). *India's fisheries boost scheme*. Retrieved February 10, 2021, from www.worldfishing.net/news101/industry-news/indias-fisheries-boost-scheme

Yea, S., & Stringer, C. (2021). Caught in a vicious cycle: Connecting forced labour and environmental exploitation through a case study of Asia – Pacific. *Marine Policy*, *134*(14), 104825. https://doi.org/10.1016/j.marpol.2021.104825

Part III

Decolonizing Management Education and Praxis Through Postcolonial Feminism

6 The Epistemology of the Toilet

Doing Class Work in Pakistan

Ghazal Mir Zulfiqar and Ajnesh Prasad

Introduction

In this chapter[1] we study the question of class-based inequality by invoking Mary Douglas' (1966) work on how members of certain groups are stigmatized as "dirty" through their discursive and ritualistic construction as *untouchable* in relation to high-status identities (Simpson & Hughes, 2020). Positing this concern within the domain of labor, we ask: What lives matter, and what lives are expendable? (Butler, 2004). And, who, by conditions entirely beyond their control, must undertake the dirtiest and most stigmatized of work? Equally, who as a matter of birthright is precluded from doing such work?

We use Joan Acker's (2006) definition to describe class-based inequality as those "enduring and systematic differences in access to and control over resources for provisioning and survival" (444). Although such resources may take on myriad, culturally situated forms, they most commonly appear as the material wealth that structures individuals into different spheres of socio-economic classes. Notwithstanding the fact that this structuring is a case of social production, over time, socio-economic classes – and the privileges, if any, associated with them – are read as being natural and, therefore, unproblematic (Bourdieu, 1984).

To study the nexus between class and inequality, we conducted a set of exercises with students at a prestigious private business school in Pakistan with the specific intent of invoking reflexivity among them related to their own class privilege. Namely, we asked students of elite socio-economic backgrounds to consider how they relate to toilet cleaners – those *untouchables* doing the most culturally denigrated of work in Pakistani society. Through this study, we sought to address two questions. First, to understand how class privilege is discursively enacted by socio-economic elites through the identity-making processes by which they make sense of self and other. Second, we wanted to investigate the possibilities of reflexivity to disrupt,

DOI: 10.4324/9781003197270-9

or otherwise undo, the reified, cultural taken-for-grantedness of class privilege. We believe privilege built upon social and economic inequalities is especially corrosive if left unquestioned in an elite business school, for its impact inevitably shows up in managerial practice and organizational cultures. This is especially important because as Joy and Poonamallee (2013) point out, management curriculums overwhelmingly follow functionalist and interpretive paradigms, as opposed to the postcolonial paradigm, which questions hierarchy and power imbalances in knowledge creation. Postcolonialism is sensitive to issues of representation (Said, 1978), marginality and voice (Spivak, 1988), and resistance (Bhabha, 1994).

Following this approach, we study class privilege and inequality by examining the perspectives and the experiences of socio-economic elites, that is, those groups "who have vastly disproportionate control over access to a resource" (Khan, 2012, p. 362). Studying elites is critical insofar as it is the "[e]lite [who] are often the engines of inequality, whether we look at the economic distribution, political power, the definition of what is culturally desirable, or access to and control over institutions that help create social knowledge" (Khan, 2012, p. 373). Extending from this premise, while research on marginalized workers has yielded significant insights on, among other social phenomena, the scope of devalued labor and, concomitantly, explanations of prevailing economic assemblages (Zulfiqar, 2019), there continues to be a dearth of management scholarship on the precise ways in which socio-economic elites configure in the propagation of inequality. Amis et al. (2017) underscore this point by arguing that it is only in studying the microfoundations of inequality – and, by extension, class privilege – that the disposition of the existing social order will be made available for critique (and, as necessary, subversion).

Before proceeding, there merits some theoretical explanation about the site that is the focus of this study: the toilet. The toilet in Pakistan, as well as in most of the rest of the Indian subcontinent, is a compelling site for empirical study, for as one commentator insightfully observes, it sets the boundaries for "cultural and biological [superiority and] inferiority" (Penner, 2013, p. 21). Our selection of the toilet is, in part, inspired by Foucault's (1980) assertion concerning the significance of studying power at its peripheral *extremities*. In this way, the toilet as a location for empirical study – especially in terms of how its users and its cleaners socially relate to one another – represents the quintessential space at which to problematize the manifestation of both discursive and institutionalized power (Munir, 2015). It reveals the ways in which power is embedded in habitual, and seemingly mundane, practices – and, as importantly, how power is done, redone, and undone. The question of power is central to this study insofar as class privilege and inequality are socially fabricated and embodied phenomena that are made tenable only through power's discursive and institutional operation (Khan, 2012). Taking these points collectively, by critiquing a set of social interactions related to the toilet, we illuminate the subversive power of knowledge that is produced at the most marginal of sites. As educators, we use reflexive questioning to raise student consciousness about an everyday site that gives existence to their own and to others' social situatedness (Adler, 2016).

This study contributes to our understanding of how class privilege perpetuates inequality. We employ Douglas to show how certain groups are constructed as *untouchable* in relation to not just high-status identities but also to spaces considered dirty. This form of social organization solves the awkward problem of making low-status groups responsible for purifying dirty spaces such as toilets for the use of high-status groups. Our findings also demonstrate that rendering marginalized worker subjectivities invisible allows for the perpetuation of inequality, for how can what cannot be seen, felt, or heard be given recognition? Finally, while our exercises were conducted in a unique context, we believe our findings have broader pedagogical implications. Specifically, we demonstrate that it is possible to disrupt entrenched social boundaries through reflexive pedagogical approaches, so that students become a witness to their own elite privilege, are driven to question it, and move toward breaking down the oppressive hierarchies that keep marginalized people in place.

Matter Out of Place

In *Purity and Danger: An Analysis of the Concepts of Pollution and Taboo* (1966 [2002]) Douglas explicates how the matter of (im)purity determines what is culturally valued and what is culturally stigmatized. Originally published more than four decades ago, it represents one of the most important texts in the field of cultural anthropology. Through this work (and others [e.g., Douglas, 2001]), Douglas offered a cultural analysis of shared meaning and social solidarity, allowing researchers across disciplines to discover new ways of making sense of the everyday mundanities of social life (Fardon, 2007). Douglas contends that the norms that define and prescribe what is clean and what is dirty delimit judgment about objective reality, provide scripts for behavior and interaction, and act as evaluative devices that govern daily life. *Purity and Danger* illuminates how myriad cultural rituals concerning purity and impurity discursively structure the lives of individuals who are located within a particular cultural (or religious) milieu. She uses examples from everyday practices to analyze how things become categorized as dirty, such as the placement of shoes which are considered dirty when put on the table but not when placed on the floor.

For Douglas, cultural beliefs about pollution establish the boundary conditions for social relating. Indeed, such beliefs determine the type of relations that are culturally sanctioned and "the kind of contact which are thought dangerous" (Douglas, 1966, p. 4). The culturally inscribed boundary conditions are purposeful insofar as they bring order to disorder by clearly distinguishing between who and what is ontologically constituted as being clean and, relationally, who and what is ontologically constituted as being dirty. As Douglas writes: "Ideas about separating, demarcating and punishing transgressions have as their main function to impose system on an inherently untidy experience" (5).

Douglas suggests that beliefs about purity and impurity perform to organize social life by establishing the criteria that regulate how subjects relate to others with whom they cohabit cultural space. This point is further elaborated in her discussion concerning the significance of dirt in establishing the social order. Douglas explains, "[d]irt was created by the differentiating activity of mind, it was a by-product of the creation of order" (198). Thus, dirt is not, in terms of any ontological basis, a matter that is unclean; rather, it is a matter that is only culturally attributed as unclean. In being culturally attributed as unclean, the idea of dirt enables social ordering. Furthermore, Douglas reminds us that this social ordering is fraught in questions of morality as cultural rituals and symbols are invoked in the production and the reproduction of social relations and in the social assignment of, to borrow her well-recited phrase, "matter out of place."

In sum, Douglas identifies how cultural beliefs about pollution serve a regulatory purpose. It governs the subjects of a culture by demarcating what is to be considered clean versus dirty, pure versus impure, and sacred versus profane. The bifurcation of these concepts achieves two outcomes, which ultimately function to scaffold the prevailing social order (Rauf et al., 2019). First, it allows for the neat cultural ordering of individuals into a set of prescribed social hierarchies. This cultural ordering positions some individuals to occupy privileged spaces while, concomitantly, relegating other individuals to marginalized spaces. Second, though as importantly, once these bifurcated concepts become embedded within a culture, they perform, almost tautologically, to justify the social institutions that maintain the cultural ordering. In doing so, it establishes the idea that cultural ordering based on who ought to be considered pure or impure, is natural, impervious, and unproblematic – and thus, not meriting critique or subversion. Douglas' ideas are critical for conceptualizing how meanings of self and other manifest, and are negotiated, at sites that are culturally marked as being dirty versus clean.

Methods

Our study seeks to answer two research questions. First, how is class privilege discursively enacted by socio-economic elites through the identity-making processes by which they make sense of self and other? Second, what are the possibilities for reflexivity in educational settings to disrupt, or otherwise undo, the reified cultural taken-for-grantedness of class privilege? Adopting an interpretive approach, we applied qualitative research methods to collect our data and used the principles of grounded theory to theorize our findings (Glaser & Strauss, 1967; Deetz, 1983; Gioia et al., 2013).

Context and Setting

Historically, Pakistani society has been governed by the *biraderi* system. *Biraderi* refers to the kinship system in the country and explains how it stratifies society through caste-based discrimination, though it also incorporates class, gender, and religious dimensions (Javid, 2012; Lyon, 2004; Mohmand & Gazdar, 2007). Within the purview of the *biraderi* system, class and caste are often used as proxies for one other. Take, for example, the case of local Christians. Even though members of this group converted nearly two hundred years ago from Hinduism's Dalit caste, they continue to be considered low-caste *untouchables* in rural villages and urban cities alike. Far from being a relic of the time's past, *biraderi* continues to structure contemporary Pakistani society (Zulfiqar, 2019). It further merits noting that while the *biraderi* predates British imperial rule, Choi-Fitzpatrick (2017, p. 125) argues that not only did colonization leave these discriminatory structures intact, but it reified them inasmuch as it established "the caste-system as *the* organizing principle for social, political, and economic order." Postcolonial sensibilities also determine skin color preference, so that across Pakistan – as is the case for much of the Indian subcontinent – there continues to be blatant colorism (Hall, 2010; Mishra, 2015), though some argue that colorism is a proxy for other forms of discrimination in the subcontinent, particularly caste and gender (Russell-Cole et al., 2014). This is because, and not accounting for region-specific differences, low-caste people are more likely to be darker skinned than those of higher castes.

In contemporary Pakistan, cleaning arrangements are negotiated at the intersection of these social inequalities (Zulfiqar, 2019). For instance, Clarke (2003) argues that caste, class, religious identity, and occupation are inexorably linked for Christians in the province of Punjab,[2] the poorest of whom are primarily relegated to sanitation work such as toilet cleaning. In this context, toilet cleaning, in particular, is a job so stigmatized that virtually anyone who can afford to hire the services of a toilet cleaner will do so. Consequently, most middle- and upper-class individuals have never had to clean their own toilets, let alone anybody else's. In fact, not knowing how to clean a toilet is a middle- and upper-class marker of status and prestige (Pinho, 2015; Zulfiqar, 2019). This makes the toilet a peripheral but critical site of power, a site at which it is possible to study how privilege and inequality are socially and discursively woven into wider cultural and institutional structures. It is also a site where the forms of social difference discussed earlier are brought into sharp focus. Given the context, it is not surprising to have newspaper advertisements for sanitary workers (read: toilet cleaners) in public sector institutions often and explicitly state that "only non-Muslims need to apply" (Christian Today, 2013). Such an overt prerequisite for the job captures how the act of toilet cleaning relies on social boundaries related to religion – and, by extension, caste, and class. As such, the toilet can be considered a socio-political space in which two distinct sets of actors operate: the makers of the mess and the cleaners of it.

Research Design

To study the nexus between privilege and inequality that the toilet represents, we conducted a set of exercises with two undergraduate cohorts. The business school draws the majority of its student body from the country's socio-economic elite, as the tuition is prohibitively expensive for the average citizen. Each cohort included a mix of sophomores, juniors, and seniors. The 2016 cohort consisted of 31 students, with 24 women and seven men, while the 2017 cohort consisted of 48 students, with 34 women and 14 men.

The multi-component research project required students to write a 1,000- to 1,500-word personal reflection that placed toilets at the center of an interrogation about privilege and power, on the one hand, and vulnerability and stigma, on the other. The second project component asked students to conduct an in-depth interview with a cleaner whose job specifically included cleaning toilets. The third and final component involved the analysis of interview findings, synthesized into a single presentation, that would culminate in a set of policy recommendations on the issues surrounding domestic and public cleaning work.

For this chapter, we draw upon the students' personal reflections as well as a survey conducted a little over two years after the students of the second cohort finished their projects, we posted a survey on the University's student and alumni Facebook page. The survey was designed to gauge whether the project had any enduring outcomes in terms of consciousness-raising on the students who had taken the course. We received 12 responses. which allowed us to ascertain whether the project engendered any long-term effects on the students who participated in the project.

Findings Rural and Urban Elite Privilege

As mentioned earlier, the students in each cohort, like the rest of the University, overwhelmingly represent the country's upper-middle and upper class. Their reflexive essays provide powerful social commentaries on power and privilege, on the one hand, and stigma and lowliness, on the other. Those belonging to rural landowning families, in particular, described stark inequalities between their families and the villagers working for them. They described how they control all economic activity on their agricultural lands, for the entire village is often part of their estate, and every villager their actual or potential "*servant.*"

Students from larger cities, such as Lahore, Karachi, and Islamabad, shared images of privilege that were considerably less grand. Nevertheless, a recurrent theme in the student reflections was disgust at the prospect of sharing a toilet with someone else, for most had enjoyed private bathrooms at home, which often did not need to be shared even with other family members. The shared bathroom was clearly a taboo site. Many female students, in particular, disclosed that they never use public toilets. Nearly every student made a point to emphasize that the domestic workers their families hired were not allowed to use their facilities. The rural elite expect their cleaners to defecate in a bush behind their mansions, while those living in urban bungalows have a small unisex toilet built outside their homes intended for shared use by male and female domestic workers. The outside toilets are completely different from the opulent bathrooms inside the bungalows, often missing a sink and nearly always with a squat toilet instead of a water closet.

Cultural Stigmatization in Constructing the Other

The student reflections included striking accounts of stigmatization, and it became clear that this was based on the workers' class, caste, gender, religious identity, and the color of their skin, all of which became implicated in their work. The way this stigmatization was operationalized came out vividly in the complex and often bravely articulate accounts of the students' own and their families' biases and prejudices. A student described how a newly hired child worker was made to sit on the floor of the car, while the family dog occupied the seat next to the employer's children, during a long car ride that brought the worker from the village to the city.

The most worrisome aspect from the privileged family's perspective concerning the inevitable exchange between employers and workers seemed to involve the fear of being touched by the stigmatized other. One student wrote that as a child, he once refused to shake hands with a domestic cleaner, who responded poignantly by saying that she understood that he would not touch her because she cleaned toilets. Another young man wrote that as an adolescent, he would worry that the women hired to clean his bathroom would touch his toothbrush, for he felt that toilet cleaners were inherently dirty. A young woman described her contested feelings as she said a final goodbye to the woman who had worked for the family since she was a little girl. When the worker kissed her cheek in farewell, the student said she simultaneously felt choked up with emotion and contaminated by her touch.

Invisible Subjectivities

The essays described in painstaking detail how the toilet cleaners' stigmatization rendered their subjectivity largely invisible to those whom they served. Another young woman wrote that she would call the women cleaning the bathrooms in her school "*invisible fairies*" for they stayed in the bathrooms all day, hidden from view busy cleaning up after the students. The only time they could come out was during their tea break when they would sit by the bathroom door. She used the same romanticized term when describing the woman who cleaned the bathrooms at her home. A student described a conversation with a janitor, in which he learned that the latter felt the reason students did not acknowledge his existence was because they were afraid that he would try to shake their hand. He further lamented that he realized just how abhorrent the idea of shaking his hand was for the students. Some male students admitted that they did not even know the names of the women who cleaned their bathrooms at home, and a few said that they do not recall ever having had a conversation with them.

Rationalizations

One of the most striking aspects of the reflective exercise was to see how students, and their families, attempted to rationalize the stigmatization and the invisibilization that their cleaners were made to bear. A student described her own outrage when a cleaner's child used her bathroom, for she felt this made the space impure for her use. She wrote that she pushed away her feelings of guilt and embarrassment by telling herself that this was possessiveness not prejudice. Even though this particular reflection demonstrated some level of reflexivity, others wrote it was justified to prevent their domestic workers from using their bathrooms because they felt that their standards of hygiene were low. Several students documented the explanations their families gave them when they questioned them about the way their domestic employees were being treated. A young man from the rural elite wrote that he once protested with his family about hiring child workers for their estate and was told that they were saving the poor children by giving them work. This seemed to satisfy him when in fact he should have questioned this reasoning, for his family owned all the land in the village and, owing to this fact, was also responsible for all the employment in the area.

Interrogating Complicity Reflexively

The project memo that was shared with students asked them to "reflect on toilets as spaces that connote privilege, power, prestige as well as vulnerability, lowliness, and stigma." They were urged to share their stories around the toilets in their homes and outside, how they viewed the people who cleaned them, the extent to which they could empathize with them (if at all), and if they knew what kind of toilets the cleaners themselves were using. The memo referred to the toilet as a political space and asked students to consider the power dynamics between those that used it and those who cleaned it.

The project idea was received with silence and blank faces in the classroom. In their essays, several students mentioned how they had balked when they first heard that the class project for a 300-level undergraduate course would focus on toilets. One student wrote: "*The topic of this assignment alone made me uncomfortable. The word 'toilet' makes me cringe, and its synonyms aren't any better; not ladylike enough to warrant mention.*" Other students stated that they had never given toilets or toilet cleaners a second thought until these exercises forced them to write about them.

Many students admitted that while writing their reflections they began to recognize how their families made invisible the "*vast army of workers*" that they employed, treating them as "*social waste,*" rather than recognizing them as "*humans who have the same political and social rights as us, human who have their own wants and needs, humans who have their own dreams.*" Other students noticed and pointed out the specific inequalities that were used to distance workers. Another student wondered what exactly it was with language that appeared to lend more dignity to a worker depending on what words were used to address her, and described how she switched from calling her domestic worker "*safai waali*" or cleaning woman to "*maid,*" admitting that she was not sure how appropriate was the latter term. Others, however, recognized that respectful words of address could not hide the hypocrisy with which their families treated their workers. One exclaimed that she shuddered at the stark inequalities built into her family home when she realized that while her family had several bathrooms and even a powder room meant only for guests, the one-room quarter of their domestic worker – who had worked for them for some 30 years and who the family referred to as a family member – was allotted included only a squat toilet without walls.

The reflections included powerful testimony into how the project was raising consciousness among young people of privilege about the social inequalities from which they benefitted though to which they paid no attention. A young woman admitted: "*Very late in my life did I associate a clean, spacious, functional bathroom with privilege, having been previously barely conscious of the possible social and political realities it embodies.*" Another student talked about her own transformation and how she believed this could lead to wider social change and possibly even policy action. Other students placed the discomfort they felt at discovering the acute inequalities they had been a party to in wider context, questioning the role education, parenting, and social norms had played in the unconscious behavior they had exhibited toward those that cleaned their excretory waste.

When the students, all of whom have since graduated, were sent a survey regarding the class project and asked whether it had any enduring impact on them, the ones that responded, stated that an intervention was necessary to improve the conditions of work for domestic and public cleaners. The majority said that they were shocked to learn about the *"casual breach"* of worker rights and most shared findings from their class project with family and friends.

Other students said that their friends were astonished to find out that toilet cleaners have aspirations similar to their own, such as desiring an education for their children. One student wrote of her surprise when she learned that workers knew just how hazardous were the cleaning products they were being made to use, but that they did not protest for fear of being fired. She said this dispelled her earlier assumption that cleaners were inherently irresponsible and ignorant. Ultimately, these realizations functioned to disrupt us-versus-them attitudes. One student wrote that the most important lesson that the exercise taught her was to proffer respect to those that cleaned her mess.

More than half the students responding to the survey said that they now talk to cleaners to learn more about their lives and that it had changed their behavior toward toilet cleaners in both public and domestic spaces. One respondent wrote: "*I have stopped pretending that they are invisible. I make sure to say hello or acknowledge their presence and the difference that it makes in my life.*" Another wrote that she had never imagined she could clean her own bathroom, but now she tries to help her domestic worker, and when the latter protests, she tells her that it is not her job to clean somebody else's mess.

Discussion

Our study considered class, privilege, and social inequality. Specifically, we explore how class privilege and social inequality are discursively and culturally produced through the concomitant processes by which subjects make sense of self and the stigmatized Other. The findings also show how reflexive engagements with consciousness-raising make visible the boundaries upon which class privilege rests and moves students toward subversion actions intended to catalyze meaningful social change.

Class privilege and social inequality

The *biraderi* system in Pakistan, much like in the rest of the Indian subcontinent, divides society into caste-based hierarchies, which are informed by myriad class, gender, and religious identities (Bapuji & Chrispal, 2020; Zulfiqar, 2019). The student reflections that emerged from the class exercises uncovered stark social and economic inequalities. Douglas (2002) contends that there is a moral order to rituals and symbols that are used in the production and reproduction of social relations. The student essays provided numerous examples of how the privileged are socialized to distance themselves from their "servants," which ultimately established a largely impervious cultural boundary between constituents of different classes of people. Their acts of distancing serve as a ritualistic initiation into the subservience expected of the other, therein capturing Douglas' (2002) observation about how myriad cultural performances are enacted along the fault lines of impurity and contamination to create and maintain the parameters of social relating between different classes of people.

In the local culture, the toilet is a taboo site, particularly the one that is shared by strangers (as in the case of public bathrooms) or by those of an inferior status (in the case of private toilets) – for here the purity of the self is threatened by the imprint of those whose identities are perceived as less pure (Douglas, 2002). The reflective essays reveal the cultural notion that toilets are such dirty spaces that the people cleaning them are dirtied by association (Ashforth & Kreiner, 1999). To return to Douglas' metaphorical illustration of shoes on the table versus shoes on the floor, the toilet is socially constructed as a space too dirty to clean for the privileged class, but not too dirty to clean when it comes to the individuals doing such work for, based on their caste, class, and religious identities, their subjectivities are culturally positioned as being ontologically impure.

At the same time, while the cleaners are meant to clean their employers' toilets, they are not permitted to use them. This extends the notion of dirt beyond Douglas' theorizing in *Purity and Danger* (2002), for here is a case of members of a marginalized group being expected to clean a space constructed as too dirty for the privileged to clean, but not dirty enough that the marginalized should be allowed to use it. Such cultural attributions are tantamount to constructing their identities as being dirtier than the very toilets they are tasked to clean.

Legitimation is a key mechanism for perpetuating the authority of the privileged while reducing resistance from non-dominant groups (Costa-Lopes et al., 2013). The most dominant legitimizing discourse the student reflections uncovered pertained to disease and hygiene. Poverty is another commonly used excuse, especially when it comes to hiring child workers, who the elite reason will "*die if they were left with their poor parents.*" Another rationalization is that toilet cleaning, though stigmatized, is after all a paid job, that allows the poor to build their lives with the cash and in-kind benefits their employment provides.

Rendering the worker invisible showed to be a form of authenticating class privilege and social inequality. Many students admitted that they and their families routinely avoid physical and verbal contact with the cleaners. Making the worker invisible is also a way of dealing with the awkwardness of intimacy that is inevitable in domestic employment. Thus, making invisible *or unseeing the other* is an important mechanism for marginalizing a group's social identity and preserving existing social hierarchies that organize society.

These findings show how in our context "dirty" groups are discursively and ritualistically constructed as *untouchable* in relation not just to high-status identities but also to spaces that are themselves considered dirty, marking low-status individuals as socially dirtier than the dirtiest of spaces. This solves the cultural problem of making low-status groups responsible for purifying dirty spaces such as toilets for the use of high-status groups while at the same time preventing them from using such spaces. Second, the findings establish that making marginalized worker subjectivities invisible allows for the perpetuation of inequality, for how can what cannot be seen, felt, or heard be given recognition and legitimation (Butler, 2004)? Hence, we argue that invisibilization adds to the repertoire of inequality-producing discursive and ritual practices (Costa-Lopes et al., 2013).

Consciousness-raising

In the four months that the students were involved in the semester-long project, their initial perplexity, and discomfort at having to focus on the toilet as the object of their research, transformed into an appreciation of the acute social inequalities that the site represents. In so doing, it prompted students to recognize their own complicity in sustaining society's oppressive class structures. The design and the outcomes of this project have several noteworthy implications for management education.

The first has to do with the role of values in business school curricula (Fotaki & Prasad, 2015). When this involves teaching students from elite socio-economic backgrounds, who will predictably go on to assume careers in various managerial capacities within industry, there is a need to take seriously the criticism that business schools inculcate a set of materialistic values into students (Adler, 2016; Joy & Poonamallee, 2013). Our findings reveal that projects such as the one we describe here allow students to question not only their own social values, but also those of their families as well as the wider cultural context in which they find themselves situated. This questioning led them to a purposeful change in behavior toward those whose invisible work they realized had been supporting them, their lives, and their social positions.

The second implication of this research study has to do with the pedagogical approach. Our study shows that transformative learning occurs when the conventional "sage on the stage" approach to teaching is replaced by open and reflexive learning opportunities (Adler, 2016; Dyer & Hurd, 2016), that can upend processes of legitimation and make conventionally invisible practices visible. It occurred through a pedagogical approach informed by the postcolonial paradigm (Joy & Poonamallee, 2013), through which students were able to begin to interrogate their assumptions and complicity in reproducing the structures of inequality around them (Fotaki & Prasad, 2015). The reflexive exercises brought to the forefront social mores that robbed the workers of their personhood – for example, by exploiting their labor or rendering them invisible. Despite the *biraderi* system's entrenched social norms and the intense stigma associated with low-status identities such as those of toilet cleaners (Zulfiqar, 2019), these findings demonstrate that the project provided significant possibilities for social change by enabling students to think critically about their own class privilege and act courageously to disrupt extreme social inequalities (Adler, 2016; Turner, 2003).

In sum, given the findings that emerged from this study, we believe that it is possible for critical pedagogical approaches to dislocate culturally codified social systems considered too entrenched to change (Grey, 2004). This is especially promising for the Indian subcontinent, where the cultural codification of social inequality is too often understood to be natural and, thus, largely impervious from social change. Student reactions demonstrate that reflexive class projects have the capacity to make them conscious witnesses to their own complicity in legitimizing privilege and marginalization through discursive and ritualistic practices. It prompts them to question themselves, their families, and their elite status. Many reported being moved to action to dismantle the social boundaries that culturally negate the marginalized workers designated to clean toilets.

Notes

1. This chapter is adapted from a paper presented at the 80th Annual Meeting of the Academy of Management. An abbreviated version of the paper was published in the *Academy of Management Best Paper Proceedings* (Zulfiqar & Prasad, 2020, A much lengthier, full-length version of the study upon which this chapter is based was published in *Academy of Management Learning and Education* (Zulfiqar & Prasad, 2021).
2. The university at which we conducted our study is located in the Pakistani province of Punjab.

References

Acker, J. (2006). Inequality regimes: Gender, class, and race in organizations. *Gender and Society*, *20*(4), 441–464.

Adler, P. (2016). 2015 presidential address: Our teaching mission. *Academy of Management Review*, *41*(2), 185–195.

Amis, J., Munir, K. A., & Mair, J. (2017). Institutions and economic inequality. In R. Greenwood, C. Oliver, T. Lawrence, & R. Meyer (Eds.), *The SAGE handbook of organizational institutionalism* (2nd ed., pp. 705–736). Sage.

Ashforth, B. E., & Kreiner, G. E. (1999). "How can you do it?" Dirty work and the challenge of constructing a positive identity. *Academy of Management Review, 24*(3), 413–434.

Bapuji, H., & Chrispal, S. (2020). Understanding economic inequality through the lens of caste. *Journal of Business Ethics, 162*(3), 533–551.

Bhabha, H. (1994). Of mimicry and man. In *The location of culture*. Routledge.

Bourdieu, P. (1984). *Distinction: A social critique of the judgement of taste.* Harvard University Press.

Butler, J. (2004). *Precarious life: The powers of mourning and violence.* Verso.

Choi-Fitzpatrick, A. (2017). *What slaveholders think: How contemporary perpetrators rationalize what they do.* Columbia University Press.

Christian Today. (2013, July 25). *Pakistan's Christians and other religious minorities should take sweeper jobs, says one minister.* www.christiantoday.com/article/pakistans.christians.and.other.religious.minorities.should.take.sweeper.jobs.says.one.minister/33360.htm

Clarke, S. (2003). Conversion to Christianity in Tamil Nadu. In R. Robinson & S. Clarke (Eds.), *Religious conversion in India: Modes, motivations and meanings* (pp. 323–350). Oxford University Press.

Costa-Lopes, R., Dovidio, J. F., Pereira, C. R., & Jost, J. T. (2013). Social psychological perspectives on the legitimation of social inequality: Past, present and future. *European Journal of Social Psychology, 43*(4), 229–237.

Deetz, S. A. (1983). Critical interpretive research in organizational communication. *The Western Journal of Speech Communication, 46,* 131–149.

Douglas, M. (1966 [2002]). *Purity and danger: An analysis of concepts of pollution and taboo.* Massachusetts Institute of Technology.

Douglas, M. (2001). Dealing with uncertainty. *Ethical Perspectives, 8*(3), 145–155.

Dyer, S. L., & Hurd, F. (2016). "What's going on?" Developing reflexivity in the management classroom: From surface to deep learning and everything in between. *Academy of Management Learning & Education, 15*(2), 287–303.

Fardon, R. (2007). Dame Mary Douglas (1921–2007). *Anthropology Today, 23*(5), 25–27.

Fotaki, M., & Prasad, A. (2015). Questioning neoliberal capitalism and economic inequality in business schools. *Academy of Management Learning and Education, 14*(4), 556–575.

Foucault, M. (1980). *Power/knowledge: Selective interviews and other writings 1972–1977.* Pantheon.

Gioia, D. A., Corley, K. E., & Hamilton, A. L. (2013). Seeking qualitative rigor in inductive research: Notes on the Gioia methodology. *Organizational Research Methods, 16*(1), 15–31.

Glaser, B. G., & Strauss, A. L. (1967). *The discovery of grounded theory: Strategies for qualitative research.* Aldine.

Grey, C. (2004). Reinventing Business Schools: The Contribution of Critical Management Education. *Academy of Management Learning & Education, 3*(2), 178–186.

Hall, R. (2010). *A historical analysis of skin color discrimination in America: Victimism among victim group populations*. New York, NY: Springer Science.

Javid, H. (2012). *Class, power and patronage: The landed elite and politics in Pakistani Punjab* (PhD Thesis). London School of Economics and Political Science.

Joy, S., & Poonamallee, L. (2013). Cross-cultural teaching in globalized management classrooms: Time to move from functionalist to postcolonial approaches? *Academy of Management Learning and Education, 12*(3), 396–413.

Khan, S. R. (2012). The sociology of elites. *Annual Review of Sociology, 38*, 361–377.

Lyon, S. (2004). *An anthropological analysis of local politics and patronage in a Pakistani village*. Edwin Mellon Press.

Mishra, N. (2015). *India and colorism: The finer nuance*. Washington University Global Studies Law Review, 14. https://openscholarship.wustl.edu/law_globalstudies/vol14/iss4/14.

Mohmand, S., & Gazdar, H. (2007). *Social structures in rural Pakistan: Determinants and drivers of poverty reduction and ADB's contribution in rural Pakistan*. Asian Development Bank.

Munir, K. A. (2015). A loss of power in institutional theory. *Journal of Management Inquiry, 24*(1), 90–92.

Penner, B. (2013). *Bathroom*. Reaktion Books.

Pinho, P. S. (2015). The dirty body that cleans: Representations of domestic workers in Brazilian common sense. *Meridians, 13*(1), 103–128.

Rauf, A. A., Prasad, A., & Ahmed, A. (2019). How does religion discipline the consumer subject? Negotiating the paradoxical tension between consumer desire and the social order. *Journal of Marketing Management, 35*(5–6), 491–513.

Russell-Cole, K., Wilson, M., & Hall, R. E. (2014). *The color complex: The politics of skin color in a new millennium*. Anchor.

Said, E. W. (1978). *Orientalism*. Penguin Books.

Simpson, R., & Hughes, J. (2020). Mary Douglas: The cultural and material manifestations of dirt and dirty work. In R. McMurray & A. Pullen (Eds.), *Rethinking culture, organization and management*. Routledge.

Spivak, G. C. (1988). Can the subaltern speak? In C. Nelson & A. Grossberg (Eds.), *Marxism and interpretation of culture* (pp. 271–313). Macmillan Education.

Turner, B. (2003). Social capital, inequality and health: The Durkheimian revival. *Social Theory & Health, 1*(1), 4–20.

Zulfiqar, G. M. (2019). Dirt, foreignness, and surveillance: The shifting relations of domestic work in Pakistan. *Organization, 26*(3), 321–336.

Zulfiqar, G. M., & Prasad, A. (2020). Interrogating the toilet as a seat of power and privilege. *Academy of Management Best Paper Proceedings*. https://journals.aom.org/doi/abs/10.5465/AMBPP.2020.46

Zulfiqar, G. M., & Prasad, A. (2021). Challenging social inequality in the global South: Class, privilege, and consciousness-raising through critical management education. *Academy of Management Learning and Education, 20*(2), 156–181.

7 Bringing Postcolonial Women Writers to Executive Education

Case of Women Managers' Program in India

Nimruji Jammulamadaka and Padmavati Akella

Introduction

Feminist postcolonial scholarship is a disciplinary home to several women theorists of South Asian origin – Gayatri Chakravarty Spivak, Lata Mani, Ritu Birla, Naila Kabeer, Ania Loomba, Uzma Falak, Leela Gandhi, Chandra Talpade Mohanty, Pushkala Prasad to name a few. In adopting the critical postcolonial lens, the discipline of management and organization studies (MOS) has appropriated the fertile work of these theorists to varying degrees. While Spivak remains part of the holy trinity of postcolonial scholarship within MOS (Prasad, 2003), many others have been drawn upon to emphasize characteristics of the postcolonial space-time and/or acknowledge the third world woman as a distinct non-monolithic category within MOS. Notwithstanding these acknowledgments of the heterogeneity of third-world woman, the "occupation of concern" (Riad & Jack, 2021) within postcolonial MOS with the third-world woman, especially from South Asia, carries a particular kind of gaze. The gaze identifies her as the dominated female worker participating in global value chains, informal sector (Alamgir, 2020) or the rural/urban underprivileged, poor woman who participates in the global development industry through programs of microfinance, women's empowerment, etc. (Kabeer, 2001, 2002, 2005a). This chapter diffracts this gaze by turning its attention to women managers and aligns with scholarship focused on women managers from postcolonial contexts (Carrim & Nkomo, 2016; Muller, 1998; Nkomo & Ngambi, 2009; Paludi & Mills, 2013).

This chapter differs from other contributions to this volume in not restricting its focus to any single woman theorist/thinker/practitioner. Instead, it engages with women managers from the post-colonial Indian context specifically and with women post- and decolonial feminist writers

DOI: 10.4324/9781003197270-10

broadly. This chapter is a collaboration of two women, one of whom is the instructor in a women's leadership program, and another a participant in this program. Situating ourselves against a backdrop of executive education for women managers, we come together to reflect upon the praxis of decolonizing gender and management and the ways engagement with the "postcolonial woman" enables and strengthens the capacities of women as and beyond managers. Together, we complement the category of the woman writer, where women managers transform from mere research objects into cognizant and active participants and co-creators of knowledge. We offer insights from an executive education program for women managers, as an illustration of a decolonizing praxis where participants examined and discussed power asymmetries, post-colonial conditions, gender relations, and decolonizing by drawing upon a diverse array of women authors from post- and decolonial studies and gender studies, while enhancing their managerial skills and knowledge. The rest of the chapter is organized as follows. We first briefly introduce the focus on women managers and turn attention to executive education for women managers from a post-colonial perspective. In the next section, we provide a brief description of the executive education program TLPWE. The next section discusses participant experiences from the class. We finally conclude the chapter with some insights pertaining to post- and decolonial women's writing and women managers. In providing an account of the experiences of the participants, we draw upon conversations inside and outside the class.

Executive Education and Women Managers

A plethora of executive education programs target women following corporate diversity and inclusion policies providing training in functional management skills, leadership, communication, interpersonal, and networking. India has one of the lowest gender diversity in management with only eight per cent of women in management roles as of 2019 (Grant, 2020; Kersley et al., 2019). Consequently, both corporates and management schools have become active in providing customized women leadership and capacity-building programs, to enhance the proportion of women managers in India. This woman manager is the subject of this chapter's analysis.

Women's empowerment discourses of development management literature (Cin, 2017; Clark et al., 2019; Harcourt, 2016; Mohanty, 1991) have been critiqued for adding women into programs (Connell, 2016) and representing heterogeneous "third world woman" as "always already constituted . . . . 'powerless', 'exploited', 'sexually harassed'" (Mohanty, 2020, 2015). The subject in these discourses and critiques is the underprivileged, poor (rural or urban) woman of the third world (Kabeer, 2005b).

She informs the research of post- and decolonial feminist scholars such as Mohanty and Kabeer.

In the management literature, the third-world woman manager is largely absent as a subject. A race and location-agnostic woman manager is the subject of women in management, (Davidson, 2012; Davidson & Burke, 2000; Schein, 2007) and diversity and inclusion discourse (Henderson et al., 2013Korabik & Ayman, 1989; Nath, 2000; Rigg & Sparrow, 1994). She appears as someone who needs special inputs to tackle the apparent "deficiencies" of women (Ely et al., 2011; Henderson et al., 2013; Korabik & Ayman, 1989) and developing competence in behaving according to mas-culine management. Masculine management practices (Acker, 1990, 1992a, 1992b, 2006a, 2006b; Ely & Meyerson, 2000) continue to be seen as the norm, and women managers' capacity-building programs accept the prem-ise of "masculine" management practice. Challenges are often articulated as women's reluctance to engage in politics, limited networking opportunities owing to "boys club" (Sinclair & Ewing, 1992), need for work-life balance in order to fulfill child-bearing, parenting, and caring responsibilities (Bud-dhapriya, 2009; Chawla & Sharma, 2016; Sullivan & Mainiero, 2008). To the extent a third-world woman appears, she is frequently seen as a poor underprivileged woman subject similar to women's empowerment and development literature.

In contrast, in post- and decolonial management studies literature the subject is generally the third-world academic who is under the hegemony of Western management knowledge (Jammulamadaka et al., 2021; Faria et al., 2010; Ruggunan & Sooryamoorthy, 2018; Westwood et al., 2014), infrequently a subaltern manager and business executive who seeks to sur-vive and thrive within Western management's hegemony (Jammulamadaka, 2017; Yousfi, 2014). In the last decade, some studies by postcolonial women management scholars have turned attention to women managers in post- and decolonial locations (Muller, 1998; Ozkazanç-Pan & Clark Muntean, 2018; Ozkazanç-Pan, 2009; Carrim & Nkomo, 2016; Nkomo & Ngambi, 2009; Paludi & Mills, 2013; Paludi et al., 2020; Sposato & Rumens, 2021). Even though the post-colonial woman manager finally enters management literature, she is an object of study, whose challenges and identity work are examined by the authors.

As such women's executive education has received limited attention so far in this era of diversity and inclusion (Sullivan & Mainiero, 2008; Ely et al., 2011; Hopkins et al., 2008). Literature examining women's execu-tive education in the post-colonial context is altogether missing. Against this backdrop, reviewing executive education programs aimed at women globally, we notice that extant executive education programs for women in the West do not account for the gendered, masculine management practices of organizations. They are silent about the prevalence of patriarchy in organizations and wider society; nor do they problematize the socialization of women into the masculine norm in order to attain professional (and personal) success. Briefly reviewing executive education programs for women managers being offered in India, we notice that they are aligned with similar global programs. The race-agnostic woman manager or the intersectional woman manager who appeared briefly as the subject in post- and decolonial research on women in management or feminist management studies disintegrates amidst the content of executive education programs.

The prescriptions for addressing "women's unique challenges" through executive education, on the one hand, re-affirm masculine management as the ideal, and on the other, displace native and post-colonial gender relations and organizing practices, with Western gender relations[1]. Importing Western content and curricula of women's executive education into post-colonial contexts such as India, following the hegemony of Western management knowledge (Jack, 2015; Jammulamadaka et al., 2021; Prasad, 2003, 2012), performs a double erasure, a double omission. Not only does it omit a gendered understanding of managerial practice, but also the constitutive intersectionality of gender relations with coloniality, colonialism, and nationalism (Chatterjee, 1989; Lugones, 2010, 2016; Nandy, 1976). These erasures are particularly problematic in a post-colonial context[2] because they signify an intersection of a post-colonial society's gender relations, and organizing practices with a masculine, eurocentric management knowledge and education.

Consequently, we argue that imported executive education and capacity-building programs that offer only management skills are of limited assistance in post-colonial locations such as India in challenging the prevailing gender apartheid at work and at home, and its constitutive intersections with coloniality/modernity. One of the participants of the executive education program case study TLPWE discussed in this chapter articulated the problem as follows:

> Entrenchment of certain views around women being the weaker sex and being unfit for most roles that men perform is conveniently accepted and preached. These lines of gradual mental conditioning of women as an inferior gender group, it almost became a norm even in current societal setting for women to accept this induced standard. Women as a commune wage a daily struggle for recognition of their rights as human beings.

This woman manager echoes the feelings and experiences of women managers in other colonized locations such as South Africa (Carrim & Nkomo, 2016). Our own experiences and post- and decolonial scholarship on women managers (Carrim & Nkomo, 2016; Muller, 1998; Paludi & Mills, 2013; Paludi et al., 2020) suggest that often women executives in post-colonial locations across organizational hierarchy and industry from the front line to the C-suite executives, experience this gender apartheid of being perceived as a weaker and inferior gender as a struggle for identity. Similarly, many women executives, following societal norms, have embraced patriarchal gender relations and division of labor, undervaluing their capabilities and roles in society and at work. Consequently, women managers' pursuit of professional and personal aspirations in the form of self, family, and work-life balance are rendered as a mirage and a myth. While the challenges experienced and ideals desired by women managers have been the product of deeper socio-historical processes, executive education programs have dealt with them under the euphemism of work–life balance. This approach valorizes individual initiative around developing political and leadership skills, time management, and de-stressing, within a popular historical macro narrative that reinforces patriarchy, neo-colonialism, and globalization. It is no co-incidence that studies have identified issues related to family support and flexitime as key challenges hindering women's careers even in post-colonial contexts (Buddhapriya, 2009; Chawla & Sharma, 2016). Sidestepping the issues of identity struggles, and devoid of any appreciation for the historical and structural factors that contribute to the crises, imbalances, and struggles experienced by women managers, this approach renders women managers' pursuit of self-family and work–life balances unrealizable, reinforcing feelings of inadequacy, and ineffectiveness in realizing their ideal. It could even be argued that pursuit of careers in such contexts has left some women in a psychologically worse off condition, and this probably explains why more women have been exiting their careers in counties like India, where entry and exit of women into the workforce seems to be driven by household financial needs, more than personal fulfillment (Sarkar et al., 2019). Extant executive education programs for women managers/executives aimed at their empowerment, however, do not address this core limitation and tension, that is, gender relations and management relations as the manifestation of deeper socio-historical processes.

We suggest that executive education programs for women managers oblivious to gendered management and patriarchal relations of society are of limited assistance in post-colonial locations such as India. They are ineffective in transforming prevailing gender apartheid at work and at home, and its constitutive intersections with coloniality/modernity. Ignorance of postcolonial gendered management in executive education persists despite several celebrated women post- and decolonial feminist writers from South Asia. Postcolonial feminists such as Spivak, Chandra Mohanty, and Lata Mani, with whose names, we began this chapter, have critiqued Western feminist gender perspectives as Eurocentric – which do not recognize the diverse gender relations that have existed in various colonized societies, includ ing South Asia. They, along with others, tell us that contemporary gender relations in post-colonial locations are the effects of deeper co-constitutive socio-historical processes such as modernity/coloniality, capitalism, colonialism, nationalism, patriarchy, and globalization. But these insights have not become available to women managers of post-colonial locations, given that postcolonial perspectives have largely been understood as a critical theoretic lens rather than praxis (Jammulamadaka, et al., 2021). They are, therefore, neither part of an MBA education nor executive education programs. Even though diversity and inclusion are now being discussed within management curricula, it remains limited to the Western perspective and practice with hardly any reference to local gender relations. In this context, the current case study offers a decolonizing praxis of integrating the work of postcolonial feminist writers into women managers' executive education programs.

Case of TLPWE

The program "Transitioning into Leadership: Program for Woman Executives" (TLPWE) was launched by the Indian Institute of Management Calcutta (IIMC) in 2017. This program was designed by two women faculty, Leena Chatterjee, a professor in Organization Behavior, and Pragyan Rath, a professor in Business Communication, and delivered by a team of IIM-C faculty. This was a year-long program that aimed at sensitizing women executives, with a minimum of five years of work experience, to the transformations necessary in successfully transitioning from a managerial role to a leadership role. In responding to the question "How do women in the corporate become effective leaders . . . at various levels of managerial, administrable and political crossroads" (program webpage), the program explicitly included gender and postcolonial woman, as subjects and disciplines through which the experiences of women participants as well as functional concepts and skills taught were to be refracted. TLPWE effected a novel departure by specifically incorporating three additional aspects – first, legal perspectives for working women, second, gender issues and third, working women in emerging markets. The structuring of the program was such that working women in emerging markets and gender issues appeared at regular intervals during the program. There was a specific emphasis on postcolonial women managers. The program devoted about 20 per cent of its time to these subjects.

Postcolonial woman module: A decolonizing praxis

TLPWE provided a unique opportunity because rarely were post- and decolonial ideas being discussed in a management classroom in India, let alone in an executive education classroom. There was limited readily available pedagogic material for this purpose. Most of the literature of postcolonial feminist writers is theoretically dense and is in the field of literature and culture studies. In these circumstances, it seemed prudent to introduce participants to post- and decolonial feminist thought through a focus on everyday workplace behavior and praxis.

Accordingly, the first author developed a four-episode case study (see case "Conversations at work" of IIMC Case Center). In contrast to conventional Harvard business publishing case studies, this case was written as a drama to underscore everyday workplace behavior, with each episode featuring one meeting and a prologue and epilogue. The dialogue was drawn from regular everyday conversations that occurred in workplaces in India and involved men and women managers and employees. The idea was to use these dialogues and the behaviors of the case characters to draw participants into a discussion on the gendered nature of workplaces and eventually toward the gendered and colonized nature of management. Once participants were drawn in, the plan was to shift the focus onto a brief historicizing of gender relations in the Indian postcolonial context and its intersection with the colonial encounter. This module received tremendous traction in the classroom, which led to the development of further sessions and new pedagogic material for a management classroom. Short autobiographies portraying identity struggles of women who are/were managers, other drama/dialogue-based episodes about women's capabilities, respect, and dignity (See case Being Women, of IIMC Case Center), and border consciousness and thinking-doing were developed. Several sets of slide decks had been developed to present post- and decolonial thinking and writing in easily accessible ways through the use of images around Indian traditional and modern, men and women from folk, mythological and historical characters as portrayed in traditional paintings and sculptures, and popular media in addition to sociological and cultural analysis and concepts. The discussion then rounded off by historicizing the nature of management practice and education in India. The idea was to facilitate participants' self-awareness and enable them to locate themselves within macro-historical, structural contexts so as to unburden themselves from false expectations generated by gendered, colonizing management structures and discourses.

Classroom and participant experience

Here, we focus on the experiences and reflections of participants about TLPWE's postcolonial woman module. We draw on the ongoing conversations participants have had among themselves, and with the instructor, both inside and outside the class about the module. The second author of this chapter has herself been a participant of TLPWE. One of the first reactions this module evoked among participants was a sense of curiosity about what "postcolonial woman" meant. Quickly, engaging with the case study *Conversations at work*, opened dialogic spaces for participants to reflect upon and discuss experiences of gender bias and workplace politics. The emotionally charged discussion enabled them to disentangle gender bias from personality and communication problems. The discussion considered the effects of a gender-blind approach by looking at how participants across organizations talk about such issues under the rubric of personality and communication problems. We saw women sharing their experiences of gender bias and workplace politics and, appreciating how organizational members, both men and women, experience and practice such biases and politics. The participants, from the distance of the class discussion, were able to personalize the case, reflect inward, and examine their careers, deep-rooted issues, and the underlying implications of the alleged and popular discourses of the inferiority of women.

As first-timers to this kind of interrogation, the women managers ripped open their calm, docile burdened demeanor with a collective self-reflexivity. In this collective decolonizing praxis and theorizing, the understanding of the group unveiled within discourses of flexibility, work–life balance, and flexitime highlighting women's needs and experiences within work and life spheres, a line of arguments which always invariably lead to women donning the primary responsibility of childcare and domestic work. It led to a collective acknowledgment of the sense that it's almost a given that women have to place these aspects as their only ambitions and that for working women it is only marginally different with their professional ambitions being purportedly "unnecessary." A solidarity of being subjugated was brought forth in this decolonizing praxis. The discussions brought into the open, the introjected feelings of inadequacy, failure, and distress, and the psychological condition where they were worse off than before they had embarked on a career. Feelings of distress, guilt, and inadequacy were among the most common emotions expressed during the sessions. Being able to express these emotions without judgment and seeing them for what they were, was a liberating and empowering moment for the participating women executives.

Beyond the catharsis, class discussions also interrogated the language of equal opportunities, and gender equality. They realized that this language typically reflected upon the implicit "reference point" of a level playing field, that is, a conceptualization of equality as "same as men," so that women's individual potentials to be "same as men" can be realized. They observed this discourse of empowerment as being based on access to paid labor, and equal pay and conveyed as its main purpose the continued silencing and denial of feminine and non-paid. These interrogations led to recognitions of the contradictions of these tools and their use to silence women and misrepresent popular vernaculars.

Apart from recognizing the gendered self and organization, participants also engaged with gender relations in the post-colonial Indian context, ancient and contemporary patriarchies, and the role of the ongoing colonial encounter in highly affectively charged discussions. With small nudges, participants sensed, recognized, and/or vocalized the conditions of coloniality, in which concepts like family, and patriarchy often linked to the description of women's experiences in the West were universalized without concern for the diversity of existences, challenges, and ways of living in the Indian context, resulting in denial and silencing of institutions and women's capabilities to create and respond to their unique situations. In the context of coloniality/modernity, participants examined and discussed issues of capitalism and management, women's empowerment, gender socialization, and patriarchy. This enabled a recognition of how history had essentially become the "product of the West in its actions upon other societies." The praxis focus widened the scope of learning from their managerial selves to include biographies of their mothers and grandmothers, and their self's as wives, daughters, sisters, and mothers. They found it liberating and empowering to understand the idea of gender equality and its dynamics in current times and crucially look beyond the popular discourses in our own sociocultural context. The pervasiveness of patriarchal gender discourses was emphasized, where even women approve of such practices as a method of control and domination. Although women play a myriad of roles as mothers, sole-bread winners of a family, and as service providers to society, they still experience a number of limitations, where the discourse of "same as men," and "as good as men" devalues, undermines, and marginalizes their lived reality of women and robs them of self-esteem and dignity.

The class felt that the discussions caused a certain deflection point and had given rise to numerous unanswered questions and reflections relating to outcomes of flexible working, gender and gendered nature of organizations, but also opened cracks in this homogenous discourse to the possibilities of different gender relations and managerial relations in different contexts, especially for recognizing the colonial patriarchy and exploring liberatory means. This decolonial praxis in the classroom produced a great sense of urgency and concern within the women managers to transform prevalent masculinities. A collective sense of the need to change this outlook was felt strongly in the group. Will women be forced to retreat from their empowered personhood, or will they join with men again in some new vision of human possibility, changing the man's world which they fought so hard to enter? These emerged as pressing self-engaging reflexive questions. One of them said, "*I will go home and share these thoughts with my daughter. I want her to know and think. It will enable her, not just me.*"

Swaying between the extremes of nativism and eurocentrism, participants were able to relate to the oppression that was felt in the colonized society, especially by women. They sensed the colonial domination materialized in selectively reinscribing native cultural traditions into modernity and then transforming those cultures into "interiorized" historical inheritances. They experienced these inheritances as impinging on their bodies, minds, emotions, their lives, their multiple identities, and their families. The discussions were emotionally charged with "unspeakable things that were unspoken" (Morrison, 1988) being spoken, acknowledged, and respected. The empowering moment unveiled reflections upon relationships with their mothers and grandmothers and their families along with the implicit (de) valuing of the status that pervaded in these relationships. It also uncovered the power of the hierarchical binary as a tool of hegemonic control through the analytical bifurcation of the world between supporters and non-supporters, superior and inferior, masculine and feminine, etc.

A torrent of emotions, euphoria, affirmation, validation, acknowledgment, loss, and disappointment prevailed among the participants about their position as women managers in the current era. It enabled them to vocalize and express their feelings of inadequacy, failure, guilt, anger, frustration, emotional turmoil, and agonizing over what they thought was "selfish" careerism versus responsibilities towards family and children. Inadvertently, the sessions served to provide a safe and legitimate space where they brought out these issues into the open, examined and reasoned with them, liberating themselves from silent agonizing. The learnings and undercurrents of the postcolonial topic set a tone enabling them to question "*how all the 'uplifting' discourses along history aren't much but misplaced sense of success and hope.*" The sessions led to an appreciation for "*the longue duree of coloniality/modernity and the inflections of the patriarchal practices that have delivered us to the current times and attitudes.*" It took a while for participants to absorb this strange fiction that surrounded their lives and be ready to embrace this newfound understanding as a tool to operate efficiently across the spheres of their lives. The experiences were quite fresh, emotions quite vivid even several months after the sessions. It unleashed diverse kinds of reflexivity among the participants. While some were grappling with questions such as "*When was the last time you wondered about how our so-called "vibrant" societies came into being? When have you last thought of your identity amongst this large ecosystem? Where have you placed yourself in that ecosystem as a human being, more importantly as a woman?";* others observed that *"changing narrative of History is of no use if we can't transform our sense of what it means to live."* Yet others felt that the course inaugurated for them a line of thinking that would be useful not just at work but in their personal lives as well. For some others, it felt like wisdom a mother had to pass on to her daughter, and some mothers swore to do this.

Discussion

In this chapter, we draw attention to executive education for women managers and the need and scope for engaging with women managers on issues of feminist post- and decolonial thinking using the case study of the postcolonial woman module in the TLPWE program of IIMC. From the case, it can be seen that women managers experience their identity aspirations and struggles around reconciling their personal and professional roles and responsibilities. Feminist post- and decolonial thinking (Lugones, 2010, 2016; Mani, 1998; Mignolo & Walsh, 2018) provides cognitive resources to understand their aspirations and struggles, yet these are generally lacking in executive education serving women managers. In managerial and workplace discourses, flexible working and managing a work–life balance are issues that are routinely linked to women (Buddhapriya, 2009; Chawla & Sharma, 2016; Sullivan & Mainiero, 2008), especially women with young children and the masculine capitalist organization is taken for granted as the norm (Acker, 1990, 1992a, 1992b, 2006a, 2006b; Ely & Meyerson, 2000). The lack of knowing/thinking/understanding that enables women managers to put their position in an alternative historical perspective, either in regular management training, or in women manager-focused executive education is troubling since working women continue to be subject to the macro, popular historical narrative that valorizes patriarchy, neo-colonialism, and globalization.

We contend that any meaningful engagement with enhancing women managers' roles and leadership in corporations in post-colonial contexts such as India will require managerial training through executive education or even an MBA to initiate conversations on the macro socio-historical forces that are shaping their experiences among both women and men. These conversations can trigger reflexivity and solidarity within the women (and men) managers and enable them to chart their own liberating pathways to personal and professional excellence and mental and emotional well-being.

Bringing in such post- and decolonial feminist perspectives into the classroom will require management scholars to depart from using postcolonial feminist writers such as Gayatri Chakravarty Spivak, Lata Mani, Ritu Birla,

Naila Kabeer, Ania Loomba, Uzma Falak, Leela Gandhi, Chandra Talpade Mohanty, Pushkala Prasad as purely theoretical analysis lenses. Management scholars will need to adopt a praxis and pedagogic approach and translate the discursive political insights of postcolonial feminist scholars into participatory, emancipatory, and empowering curricula. We contend that it is necessary for academics to translate this research into praxis and engage with women (and men) managers in order to realize the liberatory potential of post- and decolonial thinking and create better worlds. It is worthwhile to note here that development and women's empowerment literature has been able to introduce discourses of gender into capacity-building programs for underprivileged women. A similar move is required even within management curricula.

This need to engage with praxis and practitioners of management, that is, managers, brings us to a related point of pedagogic methods and materials. Postcolonial scholarship in MOS has been characterized by a research mindset and there is negligible amount of pedagogic material that can be given to participants of MBA or executive education. Postcolonial feminist thinkers are affiliated with social science disciplines such as culture studies, anthropology, literature, and gender studies. Consequently, the vocabulary and writing structure of their books and journal papers are dense and inaccessible to those outside these disciplines, especially to practicing managers and MBA students who tend to understand the world in technical-functional ways. Building capacities for decolonizing will therefore require us to devote attention to developing case studies, short readings, and essays that can be consumed by students of management and practicing managers.

A further point we make here pertains to feminist post- and decolonial scholarship within MOS. In recent years, there has been a steady rise in research that has focused on women managers from post-colonial contexts. Decolonial thinking has distinguished itself with its unmistakable allegiance with praxis. However, MOS, in appropriating decolonial thinking just like postcolonial theory, has reduced it to the status of a theoretical lens and severed the praxistical lifeblood of decolonizing (Jammulamadaka et al., 2021). Engaging with practicing managers through executive education allows us to recuperate this praxistical side of decolonizing. In addition, the experiences from TLPWE also confirm for us from a practitioner's perspective the fluid and close relationship between post- and decolonial thinking. In this regard, we endorse the suggestion of Jammulamadaka et al. (2021) to consider post- and decolonial scholarships as related rather than as two distinct divergent streams of thought.

A final point we make is for the need to unsettle the category of a post-colonial woman writer. Similar to scholarship where practicing managers have written about managing in the West, there is a need for women managers from post-colonial contexts to speak up and write about their insights and experiences, to bring the challenges and strategies of survival and resistance out of the closets. This collaborative chapter is a small attempt to underscore this need and start the process. It is by going beyond the academic confines of post- and decolonial scholarship and engaging with practicing managers that one can mobilize and reappropriate the mechanisms of capitalism and colonialism to sabotage it and transform it for better worlds at scale thus realizing the transformative worlds implicit in the theorizing of feminist postcolonial women writers.

Notes

1. Western gender relations is being used in the sense of strategic essentialism of Spivak. It is being invoked in the sense articulated by Chandra Mohanty. However, we acknowledge that gender relations even in the West can be varied.
2. The hyphenated "post-colonial" is being used to indicate the time after colonization started. It does not signify the end of colonization. "Postcolonial" without the hyphen indicates the theoretical corpus.

References

Acker, J. (1990). Hierarchies, jobs, bodies: A theory of gendered organizations. *Gender & Society*, *4*(2), 139–158.

Acker, J. (1992a). From sex roles to gendered institutions. *Contemporary Sociology*, *21*(5), 565–569.

Acker, J. (1992b). Gendering organizational theory. *Classics of Organizational Theory*, *6*, 450–459.

Acker, J. (2006a). Gender and organizations. In *Handbook of the sociology of gender* (pp. 177–194). Springer.

Acker, J. (2006b). Inequality regimes: Gender, class, and race in organizations. *Gender & Society*, *20*(4), 441–464.

Alamgir, F., & Alakavuklar, O. N. (2020). Compliance codes and women workers' (mis) representation and (non) recognition in the apparel industry of Bangladesh. *Journal of Business Ethics*, *165*(2), 295–310.

Buddhapriya, S. (2009). Work-family challenges and their impact on career decisions: A study of Indian women professionals. *Vikalpa*, *34*(1), 31–46.

Carrim, N. M. H., & Nkomo, S. M. (2016). Wedding intersectionality theory and identity work in organizations: South African Indian women negotiating managerial identity. *Gender, Work & Organization*, *23*(3), 261–277.

Chatterjee, P. (1989). Colonialism, nationalism, and colonialized women: The contest in India. *American Ethnologist*, *16*(4), 622–633.

Chawla, S., & Sharma, R. R. (2016). How women traverse an upward journey in Indian industry: Multiple case studies. *Gender in Management: An International Journal*, *31*(3), 181–206.

Cin, F. (2017). *Gender justice, education and equality: Creating capabilities for girls' and women's development*. Springer.

Clark, D. A., Biggeri, M., & Frediani, A. A. (Eds.). (2019). *The capability approach, empowerment and participation*. Palgrave Macmillan.

Connell, R. (2016). Foreword. In W. Harcourt (Ed.), *The Palgrave handbook of gender and development*. Springer.

Davidson, M. J. (2012). Women in management worldwide: Progress and prospects. *Human Resource Management International Digest*, *20*(6). https://doi.org/10.1108/hrmid.2012.04420faa.012

Davidson, M. J., & Burke, R. J. (Eds.). (2000). *Women in management: Current research issues* (Vol. II). Sage.

Ely, R. J., Ibarra, H., & Kolb, D. M. (2011). Taking gender into account: Theory and design for women's leadership development programs. *Academy of Management Learning & Education*, *10*(3), 474–493.

Ely, R. J., & Meyerson, D. E. (2000). Theories of gender in organizations: A new approach to organizational analysis and change. *Research in Organizational Behavior*, *22*, 103–151.

Faria, A., Ibarra-Colado, E., & Guedes, A. (2010). Internationalization of management, neoliberalism and the Latin America challenge. *Critical Perspectives on International Business*, *6*(2/3), 97–115.

Grant, T. (2020). *Women in business 2020: Putting the blueprint into action*. www.grantthornton.global/en/insights/women-in-business-2020/women-in-business-2020-report/

Harcourt, W. (Ed.). (2016). *The Palgrave handbook of gender and development*. Palgrave Macmillan.

Henderson, L. S., Stackman, R. W., & Koh, C. Y. (2013). Women project managers: The exploration of their job challenges and issue selling behaviors. *International Journal of Managing Projects in Business*, *6*(4), 761–791.

Hopkins, M. M., O'Neil, D. A., Passarelli, A., & Bilimoria, D. (2008). Women's leadership development strategic practices for women and organizations. *Consulting Psychology Journal: Practice and Research*, *60*(4), 348.

Jack, G. (2015). Advancing postcolonial approaches in critical diversity studies. In R. Bendl, I. Bleijenbergh, E. Henttonen, & A. J. Mills (Eds.), *The Oxford handbook of diversity in organizations* (pp. 153–174). Oxford University Press.

Jammulamadaka, N. (2017). *Indian business: Notions and practices of responsibility*. India Routledge.

Jammulamadaka, N., Faria, A., Jack, G., & Ruggunan, S. (2021). Decolonising management and organisational knowledge (MOK): Praxistical theorising for potential worlds. *Organization*, *28*(5), 717–740.

Kabeer, N. (2001). Conflicts over credit: Re-evaluating the empowerment potential of loans to women in rural Bangladesh. *World Development*, *29*(1), 63–84.

Kabeer, N. (2002). *The power to choose: Bangladeshi women and labor market decisions in London and Dhaka*. Verso.

Kabeer, N. (2005a). Is microfinance a 'magic bullet' for women's empowerment? Analysis of findings from South Asia. *Economic and Political Weekly*, 4709–4718.

Kabeer, N. (2005b). Gender equality and women's empowerment: A critical analysis of the third millennium development goal. *Gender & Development, 13*(1), 13–24.

Kersley, R., Klerk, E., Boussie, A., Longworth, B. S., Natzkoff, J. A., & Ramji, A. (2019). *The CS gender 3000 in 2019: The changing face of companies.* Credit Suisse Research Institute.

Korabik, K., & Ayman, R. (1989). Should women managers have to act like men? *Journal of Management Development, 8*(6), 23–32.

Lugones, M. (2010). Toward a decolonial feminism. *Hypatia, 25*(4), 742–759.

Lugones, M. (2016). The coloniality of gender. In *The Palgrave handbook of gender and development* (pp. 13–33). Palgrave Macmillan.

Mani, L. (1998). *Contentious traditions: The debate on sati in colonial India.* University of California Press.

Mignolo, W. D., & Walsh, C. E. (2018). *On decoloniality: Concepts, analytics, praxis.* Duke University Press.

Mohanty, C. (1991). Under Western eyes: Feminist scholarship and colonial discourses. In C. Mohanty & U. Eyes (Eds.), *Power, representation, and feminist critique* (pp. 347–357). Duke University Press.

Mohanty, C. T. (2015). Under Western Eyes: Feminist Scholarship and Colonial Discourses. In Colonial discourse and post-colonial theory (pp. 196–220). Routledge.

Mohanty, C. T. (2020). Under Western Eyes: Feminist scholarship and colonial discourses 1. In Theories of race and racism (pp. 371–391). Routledge.

Morrison, T. (1988). *Unspeakable things unspoken: The Afro-American presence in American literature.* Duke University Press.

Muller, H. J. (1998). American Indian women managers: Living in two worlds. *Journal of Management Inquiry, 7*(1), 4–28.

Nandy, A. (1976). Woman versus womanliness in India: An essay in social and political psychology. *Psychoanalytic Review, 63*(2), 301–315.

Nath, D. (2000). Gently shattering the glass ceiling: Experiences of Indian women managers. *Women in Management Review, 15*(1), 44–52.

Nkomo, S. M., & Ngambi, H. (2009). African women in leadership: Current knowledge and a framework for future studies. *International Journal of African Renaissance Studies, 4*(1), 49–68.

Ozkazanc-Pan, B. (2009). *Globalization and identity formation: A postcolonial analysis of the international entrepreneur.* University of Massachusetts Amherst.

Ozkazanc-Pan, B., & Clark Muntean, S. (2018). Networking towards (in) equality: Women entrepreneurs in technology. *Gender, Work & Organization, 25*(4), 379–400.

Paludi, M. I., Barragan, S., & Mills, A. (2020). Women CEOs in Mexico: Gendered local/global divide and the diversity management discourse. *Critical Perspectives on International Business, 17*(1), 128–147.

Paludi, M. I., & Mills, J. H. (2013). Making sense of the Latin American "other": Executive women in Argentina. *Equality, Diversity and Inclusion: An International Journal, 32*(8), 732–755.

Prasad, A. (2003). *Postcolonial theory and organizational analysis: A critical engagement.* Springer.

Riad, S., & Jack, G. (2021). Tracing the Sphinx from symbol to specters: reflections on the organization of geographies of concern. *Culture and Organization, 27*(3), 240–266.

Rigg, C., & Sparrow, J. (1994). Gender, diversity and working styles. *Women in Management Review, 9*(1), 9–16.

Ruggunan, S., & Sooryamoorthy, R. (2018). *Management studies in South Africa: Exploring the trajectory in the Apartheid era and beyond.* Palgrave-Macmillan.

Sarkar, S., Sahoo, S., & Klasen, S. (2019). Employment transitions of women in India: A panel analysis. *World Development, 115,* 291–309.

Schein, V. E. (2007). Women in management: Reflections and projections. *Women in Management Review, 22*(1), 6–18.

Sinclair, A., & Ewing, J. (1992). What women managers want: Customising human resource management practices. *Human Resource Management Journal, 3*(2), 14–28.

Sposato, M., & Rumens, N. (2021). Advancing international human resource management scholarship on paternalistic leadership and gender: The contribution of postcolonial feminism. *The International Journal of Human Resource Management, 32*(6), 1201–1221.

Sullivan, S. E., & Mainiero, L. (2008). Using the kaleidoscope career model to understand the changing patterns of women's careers: Designing HRD programs that attract and retain women. *Advances in Developing Human Resources, 10*(1), 32–49.

Westwood, R., Jack, G., Khan, F., & Frenkel, M. (Eds.). (2014). *Core-periphery relations and organisation studies.* Palgrave Macmillan.

Yousfi, H. (2014). Rethinking hybridity in postcolonial contexts: What changes and what persists? The Tunisian case of Poulina's managers. *Organization studies, 35*(3), 393–421.

Index

abuse 47, 73, 75, 76, 78, 80, 83
academia 8, 12, 36, 37, 41, 48, 56
academic research 72, 80, 83, 84
academics 32, 41, 45, 46, 47, 48, 72, 74, 83, 84, 117
Afreen Huq 12, 19, 20, 22, 24, 26, 28, 30, 32, 34
agency 7, 19, 20, 21, 26, 29, 30, 33, 34, 36, 81
ahistorical 8, 55
Ajnesh Prasad 13, 91, 92, 94, 96, 98, 100, 102, 104
ancient 114
annexation 61, 62
anthropology 93, 117
anti-colonial 9, 16, 55, 57, 58, 59, 65
anti-trafficking 87
authors 7, 12, 13, 25, 26, 29, 59, 72, 107, 108
autobiographies 112
autoethnographic 55
autonomy 28, 30, 34
Ayesha Masood 13, 55, 56, 58, 60, 62, 64, 66, 68, 70
azaadi 55

backward 20, 31
Bangladesh 1, 7, 8, 10, 11, 12, 14, 19, 20, 22, 24, 25, 26, 28, 30, 33, 34, 35, 41, 43, 44, 45, 46, 48, 49, 50, 51, 73, 86, 118, 119
Bangladeshi 12, 19, 20, 23, 27, 31, 43, 44, 45, 46, 48, 120
bankruptcy 43
binary 31, 56, 115

bondage 77, 84, 87
bonded labour 14, 86, 87
Brahmin 64, 65
bricolage 59, 60
British colonial 37, 58
British India 10, 15
bureaucratic state 57, 58
business venture 44

capitalism 1, 4, 31, 39, 58, 68, 104, 111, 114, 118
caste 4, 7, 10, 13, 22, 30, 65, 75, 76, 77, 78, 83, 84, 85, 86, 87, 95, 96, 97, 101, 104
caste-based 84, 86, 95, 101
Chan- dra Talpade Mohanty 5, 106
charitable 39, 44, 45
child sexual exploitation 80
China 69, 71, 74
Christians 95, 104
Christina Stringer 11, 72
class 1, 2, 3, 4, 7, 10, 13, 20, 22, 23, 24, 26, 30, 31, 32, 78, 79, 83, 85, 87, 91, 92, 93, 94, 95, 96, 97, 99, 100, 101, 102, 103, 104, 107, 113, 114, 116, 118
colonial discourse 5, 20, 31, 68
colonialism 1, 4, 9, 10, 12, 14, 32, 57, 58, 59, 62, 66, 67, 69, 70, 71, 109, 110, 116, 118
coloniality 10, 22, 55, 58, 68, 70, 109, 110, 111, 114, 115, 120
colorism 95
communal and religious identities 10

community 9, 25, 26, 28, 30, 32, 41, 43, 56, 77, 82, 83, 87
contemporary development 20, 30
contemporary India 13, 72, 75, 77
contextual genealogy 3
contributing authors 7, 12
corporate social responsibility 12, 56, 83, 86
corruption 36, 44, 69, 76
counter-hegemonic narratives 55
cross-border repatriation 81
cultural 1, 2, 4, 9, 14, 20, 23, 27, 30, 31, 43, 46, 49, 56, 57, 62, 68, 72, 79, 92, 93, 94, 95, 97, 100, 101, 102, 103, 105, 112, 114, 115
curricula 83, 84, 102, 109, 111, 117

Dalit 77, 78, 86, 95
debt bondage 75, 78
decolonial 6, 13, 15, 55, 57, 65, 68, 72, 106, 107, 108, 109, 110, 111, 112, 114, 116, 117, 118, 120
decolonial feminist 13, 55, 106, 108, 111, 112, 116
decolonizing 1, 8, 9, 11, 12, 55, 107, 111, 112, 113, 117
decolonizing otherwise 55
democratic 33, 39, 44, 58, 61, 62
dirt 94, 101, 102, 105
discourse 14, 19, 20, 22, 25, 31, 33, 37, 38, 40, 41, 43, 61, 62, 68, 69, 70, 101, 108, 114, 120
discrimination 24, 25, 76, 77, 78, 79, 82, 84, 87, 95
disempower 47
displacement 64
diversity 3, 56, 71, 107, 108, 111, 114, 119, 120
diversity and inclusion 107, 108, 111
doctorate 2
domestic worker 99, 100
domestic workers 81, 97, 98, 105
Doshi 2, 3, 15

East India Company 75
economic growth 25, 30, 34, 78
economic opportunities 77
Elena Samonova 11, 72, 73

elite 12, 13, 36, 37, 38, 39, 40, 41, 42, 43, 44, 45, 46, 47, 48, 49, 91, 92, 93, 94, 96, 97, 98, 101, 102, 103, 105
emotional well-being 116
empirical 20, 25, 46, 92
employer–employee 3
empowerment 12, 19, 20, 21, 22, 24, 25, 26, 27, 28, 29, 30, 31, 32, 33, 34, 43, 48, 49, 61, 106, 107, 108, 110, 114, 117, 119, 120
entrepreneur 120
entrepreneurship 9, 20, 43, 56
epistemological 67
ethnicity 10, 63
ethnocentric 31
ethnocidal genocide 67
eurocentric 109
European fascism 65
ex-colonized 2, 4, 7, 56
executive education 13, 107, 108, 109, 110, 111, 112, 116, 117
exploitation 12, 13, 72, 73, 74, 75, 76, 77, 78, 79, 80, 83, 84, 85, 86, 87, 88

fair wages 80
Falak 13, 14, 59, 60, 61, 66, 67, 69
falsehood 62
familial 26, 28, 55, 58, 59, 65
family narrative 65, 66
Farooq Ahmad 12, 36, 38, 40, 42, 44, 46, 48, 50
female 13, 23, 26, 38, 43, 46, 81, 97, 106
female workers 46
feminism 1, 2, 3, 4, 5, 6, 7, 8, 9, 14, 15, 16, 31, 34, 120
feminist 1, 2, 3, 4, 5, 6, 7, 8, 9, 10, 11, 13, 14, 15, 16, 19, 20, 23, 24, 25, 30, 34, 55, 109, 111, 112, 116, 117, 118, 120
feminist theories 20
feminization 28, 84
First-World 5, 14

Gayatri Spivak 5, 11, 12, 16, 36, 37, 39, 41, 43, 45, 47, 49, 51
gender apartheid 109, 110
gender division 1, 10
gender equality 24, 25, 30, 36, 81, 113, 114

gender gap 21
gender hierarchies 24
gender issues 111
gender-neutral 24
gender perspectives 111
geopolitical 12, 55, 57, 60, 61
globalization 74, 83, 110, 111, 116
Global North West 56
Global Slavery Index 75, 76, 81, 82, 85
Global South East 56
global value chains 29, 73, 87, 106
Grameen Bank 43, 49
guilt 48, 61, 62, 63, 68, 98, 113, 115
Gujranwala 64

handicap 7
hegemony 3, 56, 108, 109
heterogeneities 67
Hindu 24, 37, 63, 64, 85, 87
Hinduism 76, 95
Hindu women 37
historic 39, 58
historical phenomenon 74, 84
Hitler 65
homogenous 68, 114
human rights 10, 14, 39, 43, 46, 73, 82, 87
hybridity 56, 68, 72, 121

illegal immigration 57
illiteracy 79
imaginaries 57, 67
imperialism 1, 4, 6, 9, 15, 31, 32, 37, 38, 50, 56, 65, 68, 69, 70
imperialistic 5, 46
inclusion 3
independence 24, 56, 64, 65, 75
India 1, 2, 3, 5, 7, 8, 9, 10, 11, 12, 13, 14, 37, 42, 50, 58, 61, 62, 63, 64, 65, 66, 69, 70, 71, 72, 73, 74, 75, 76, 78, 79, 80, 81, 82, 84, 85, 86, 87, 104, 106, 107, 109, 110, 111, 112, 113, 115, 116, 117, 118, 119, 120, 121
Indian government 76
Indianness 65
Indians 3
Indian subcontinent 75, 92, 95, 103
Indian women 118, 120
interdisciplinary 56
international policy 30

intra-household 26, 48
intrahousehold 33
invisibilization 98, 102

Kabeer 12, 14, 19, 20, 21, 22, 23, 24, 25, 26, 27, 28, 29, 30, 31, 32, 33, 34, 106, 107, 108, 120
Kashmir 10, 13, 55, 59, 60, 61, 62, 63, 64, 65, 66, 69, 70, 71, 72
Kashmiri 13, 55, 58, 59, 60, 61, 62, 63, 64, 65, 66, 69
Kashmiri azaadi 66
Kashmiri language 60
Kashmiri Pandit 63, 64, 65
Kashmiri people 58, 61, 62, 63
Kashmiris 59, 61, 62, 63, 64, 65, 66, 72

labour 50, 80, 85, 86, 87
lamb 64
language 2, 20, 47, 55, 57, 64, 66, 67, 77, 99, 113
leadership 16, 31, 65, 107, 110, 111, 116, 119, 120, 121
leader–team 3
legitimacy 27, 36, 45, 49, 50
liberalization 28, 75, 78
liberation 24, 70, 78, 85
linear history 59
literature 8, 11, 13, 61, 73, 83, 84, 108, 112, 117, 120
loans 42, 43, 44, 119

majoritarian 57
management education 13, 14, 102, 105
Management and Organization Studies 1, 8, 11
management training 116
marginal 8, 45, 79, 93
marginalized 1, 13, 31, 36, 42, 46, 49, 57, 77, 78, 92, 93, 94, 101, 102, 103
marginalized groups 49, 77
masculine 61, 65, 108, 109, 115, 116
Maya women 6
memorialization 55, 60, 66
memoryscapes 59, 65, 66, 68
microcredit 23, 41, 42, 43, 44, 48, 50
migrant workers 2, 74, 76, 78, 81
migratory 64, 65
militaristic 57
militarized 58, 59

mimicry 56, 104
minorities 7, 57, 58, 65, 79, 104
minority 63, 77
modern slavery 13, 72, 73, 74, 75, 76, 77, 78, 80, 81, 82, 83, 84, 85, 86, 87
multidisciplinary approaches 56
multilingual 68
multinational corporations 36, 39, 50, 87
multinational enterprises 73, 75
Muslims 64, 65, 79, 96
Mussolini 65
myth 67, 72, 110
mythological 112

Naila Kabeer 11, 12, 19, 21, 23, 25, 27, 29, 31, 32, 33, 35, 106, 117
nationalism 22, 24, 57, 61, 62, 109, 111, 118
nationalistic 60, 62
nationhood 59
neoclassical 30
neocolonial 36, 37, 39, 40, 41, 47, 48, 56
neocolonialism 57
neo-colonizers 3, 7
neoliberal 15, 37, 38, 39, 41, 43, 104
New Zealand 33, 72, 75
NGO 36, 39, 40, 41, 42, 43, 44, 45, 47, 48
Nimruji Jammulamadaka 13, 106, 108, 110, 112, 114, 116, 118, 120
non-monolithic 106

ontological 57, 94
ontology 56
oppression 1, 6, 8, 31, 58, 61, 62, 66, 73, 115
organizational behavior 83
organizational studies 73, 74, 84

Padmavati Akella 13, 106, 108, 110, 112, 114, 116, 118, 120
Pakistan 1, 2, 7, 8, 10, 11, 12, 13, 14, 16, 58, 60, 61, 62, 63, 66, 68, 70, 87, 91, 92, 95, 101, 104, 105
Pakistani 60, 61, 62, 68, 70, 91, 95, 105
Pandits 63, 65
paradisiacal 60

paradox 49, 63, 65, 66
paradoxical 105
patriarchal 13, 20, 21, 22, 23, 24, 26, 27, 28, 31, 34, 43, 58, 61, 110, 114, 115
patriarchal gender discourses 114
patriarchy 1, 4, 9, 13, 21, 28, 30, 37, 38, 86, 109, 110, 111, 114, 116
peasant workers 37
pedagogic 112, 117
pedagogical 13, 93, 103
philosophical 8, 47
postcolonial 1, 2, 3, 4, 5, 6, 7, 8, 9, 10, 11, 12, 13, 14, 15, 16, 19, 20, 22, 30, 32, 49, 50, 55, 56, 57, 58, 59, 63, 66, 67, 68, 70, 71, 72, 78, 92, 103, 105, 106, 107, 108, 111, 112, 113, 115, 116, 117, 118, 120, 121
postcolonial critique 56, 70, 119
postcolonial feminism 2, 3, 4, 5, 6, 7, 8, 9, 11, 12, 13, 14, 121
postcolonial feminist 4, 5, 6, 7, 8, 9, 10
postcolonial feminist researchers 4, 8, 9
postcolonial scholarship 106
poverty 14, 19, 25, 40, 41, 42, 43, 50, 51, 64, 77, 78, 80, 81, 84, 87, 105
power dynamics 9, 31, 57, 99
pre-colonial 58
Prime Minister 64
private sector 23, 76
purdah 26

race 1, 4, 10, 30, 31, 70, 103, 108, 109, 118
racialized 3, 65
radical politics 56
randomista 24, 34
randomized control trials 24
Rashedur Chowdhury 36, 38, 40, 42, 44, 46, 48, 50
reflexivity 91, 94, 98, 113, 115, 116
rehabilitation 81, 86, 87
religion 1, 4, 7, 10, 22, 60, 63, 78, 96, 105
religious identity 95
remuneration 80

Sadhvi Dar 13, 55, 56, 58, 60, 62, 64, 66, 68, 70, 72
sati 37, 120

scholarships 117
secularism 24
self-determination 58
self-esteem 114
sexually harassed 107
skin color 3, 95
slavery 13, 14, 72, 73, 74, 75, 76, 77, 78, 80, 82, 83, 84, 85, 86, 87
social conditions 79
social dependency 24
social developments 19
socialism 24
socialization 109, 114
social relations 4, 31, 94, 101
social responsibility 12, 68
socioeconomic 75, 78
socio-economic inequalities 36, 91, 92, 94, 96, 102
socio-historical 110, 111, 116
socio-political 37, 96
solidarity 3, 4, 15, 34, 50, 59, 61, 62, 63, 65, 66, 67, 70, 93, 113, 116
South Africa 69, 71, 110, 118, 121
South African 118
South Asia 14, 22, 23, 24, 32, 33, 72, 73, 78, 86, 87, 106, 111, 119
spectacle 61
Spivak 2, 4, 5, 6, 8, 10, 12, 14, 15, 16, 36, 37, 38, 39, 41, 42, 43, 46, 47, 49, 50, 51, 92, 105, 106, 111, 116, 118
state-sanctioned narratives 59, 65
stigmatization 97, 98
subaltern 1, 5, 6, 7, 10, 12, 14, 16, 36, 37, 38, 39, 40, 41, 42, 45, 47, 48, 49, 50, 105, 108
subalternity 1, 10, 12, 37, 39, 48 *
subjugation 56, 58
sustainability 81
Swati Nagar 13, 72, 74, 76, 78, 80, 82, 84, 86, 88

taboo 97, 101, 104
textile industry 80
third world 5, 8, 10, 49, 51, 106, 107
threat 8, 26, 63, 77
TLPWE 107, 109, 111, 112, 113, 116, 117
toilets 93, 95, 96, 97, 99, 101, 102, 103

trade unions 29, 45, 51
transgenerational 56
transnational 32, 58
transnational corporations 58
tribalism 24

underprivileged 77, 106, 108, 117
unethical 42, 46
unitary identity 57
universities 44, 46
unpaid 23, 26, 79
untouchable 77, 91, 93, 102
upper caste 63
urban migrant 2, 3
Urdu 64
Uzma Falak 11, 13, 55, 59, 106, 117

values 20, 21, 22, 27, 28, 38, 40, 43, 102
veil 43
victims 21, 31, 45, 59, 75, 81, 84, 86
Vijayta Doshi 1, 2, 4, 6, 8, 10, 12, 14, 16
violation 73
violence 15, 21, 26, 28, 38, 39, 44, 48, 49, 55, 58, 59, 63, 64, 65, 66, 67, 68, 74, 81, 104
violent 27, 38, 67
visibility 55
vision 4, 6, 27, 114
voice 7, 20, 28, 29, 37, 39, 41, 46, 47, 92
vulnerable 27, 36, 41, 48, 67, 74, 76, 78, 80, 81, 82, 84, 86
vulnerable social identities 36

wage 21, 26, 79, 81, 109
Wagha border 2
western-centric 5
westerners 19
western feminism 4, 14, 32
widow 37
women 1, 2, 3, 4 5, 6, 7, 8, 9, 10, 11, 12, 13, 14, 19, 20, 21, 22, 23, 24, 25, 26, 27, 28, 29, 30, 31, 32, 33, 34, 36, 37, 38, 43, 55, 59, 61, 70, 72, 78, 79, 80, 81, 84, 85, 96, 97, 98, 106, 107, 108, 109, 110, 111, 112, 113, 114, 115, 116, 117, 118, 119, 120, 121

women executives 110, 111, 113
women managers 13, 106, 107, 108,
    109, 110, 111, 112, 113, 114, 115,
    116, 117, 120, 121
women's studies 3
women writers 2, 7, 11, 13,
    14, 118
worker rights 100
working conditions 73, 76, 79, 80
working women 23, 111, 113, 116

work-life balance 108
workplace 46, 50, 71, 79, 80, 82,
    112, 113

young man 97, 98
young woman 97, 98, 99

Zameen 61
Zulfiqar 13, 14, 91, 92, 94, 95, 96, 98,
    100, 101, 102, 103, 104, 105

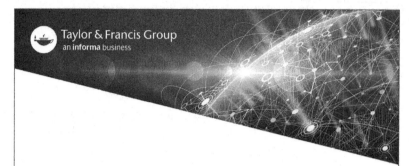

Printed in the United States
by Baker & Taylor Publisher Services